Teaching Social Studies: Portraits From the Classroom

Vincent Rogers
Arthur D. Roberts
Thomas P. Weinland
Editors

National Council for the Social Studies
Bulletin No. 82
ISBN 0–87986–057–x

NATIONAL COUNCIL FOR THE SOCIAL STUDIES

Library of Congress Catalog Card Number: 88–062522
ISBN 0–87986–057–x
Copyright © 1988 by
NATIONAL COUNCIL FOR THE SOCIAL STUDIES
3501 Newark Street N.W., Washington, D.C. 20016

TABLE OF CONTENTS

CONTRIBUTORS   v

INTRODUCTION   vii

**Chapter 1. FOLLOWING OUR FOREBEARS' FOOTSTEPS:
      FROM EXPEDITION TO UNDERSTANDING**   1
Caroline S. Donnan
      3d grade; New England colonial history; inquiry approach;
      reflections on curriculum development and evolution.

**Chapter 2. MY NAME IS ALICE: A 5TH GRADE STUDY OF
      NAMING AND FAMILY HISTORY**   10
Alice Seletsky
      5th grade; using study of students' names as a group-forming
      exercise at the beginning of the school year; multidisciplinary/
      humanities.

**Chapter 3. HONOR THE EARTH: LEARNING FROM NATIVE
      AMERICANS**   19
Mari DeRoche
      3d grade; ecology through study of Native American cultures;
      cooperative learning.

**Chapter 4. INTEGRATION: AN INFORMAL APPROACH TO
      TEACHING PRIMARY SOCIAL STUDIES**   28
Lise Melancon and Suzanne Peters
      K–2d grade; interdisciplinary, thematic one-year curriculum; uses
      archaeological dig as core.

Chapter 5. WHERE HAVE ALL THE HEROES GONE?   36
Jessie B. Crook
      6th grade; role-playing and biography.

**Chapter 6. THE MAKING OF A CONSTITUTION: SELF-
      GOVERNMENT 7TH GRADE STYLE**   42
Betsy Dudley
      7th grade; curriculum and cooperative learning about the
      Constitution; responsibility; group process.

**Chapter 7. THINKING, VIEWING, AND DECIDING:
      STRATEGIES IN UNITED STATES HISTORY**   49
Kevin O'Reilly
      High school; curriculum for developing critical thinking and
      decision making; developing classrooms conducive to inquiry.

Chapter 8.   TEACHING ABOUT THE VIETNAM WAR   61
Michael Huff and Stuart B. Palonsky
  High school; United States history; curriculum and personal
  reflections on teaching about Vietnam.

Chapter 9.   OPENING MOUTHS AND OPENING MINDS:
  THE AMERICAN EXPERIENCE PROGRAM   68
John Rossi
  High school; United States history; 20-year evolution of a
  curriculum; conceptual; inquiry- and activity-based.

Chapter 10. SOCIOLOGY AND SOCIAL RESEARCH: A
  RURAL-URBAN EXCHANGE   77
Pauline U. Dyson
  11th–12th grade; sociology; describes student-directed inquiry
  into current social problems using student exchange.

Chapter 11. TEACHING ECONOMICS IN THE
  INFORMATION AGE: CHALLENGES AND
  OPPORTUNITIES   86
John Driscoll
  12th grade; government and economics; computer applications;
  partnerships with business; cooperative "intrapreneurial" project.

CONCLUDING COMMENTS   94

CONTRIBUTORS

Jessie B. Crook is the Curriculum Coordinator at the Mifflin International Middle School in Columbus, Ohio. She has made presentations at local and state social studies conferences, at the National Association of Middle Schools, and to classes at Ohio State University. She has contributed to *The Review,* published by the Ohio Council for the Social Studies.

Mari DeRoche teaches at the Charter Oak Neighborhood School in West Hartford, Connecticut. She has taught grades 3–6. Her curriculum, "Honor the Earth, Learning from Native Americans," was recipient of a 1987 Connecticut Celebration of Excellence Award. She has a state grant to produce a film on Native Americans in Connecticut.

Caroline S. Donnan is Coordinator of Admissions Outreach at Middlebury College. She is the recipient of local, state, and international awards for exemplary educational practices. Her work has been the model for interdisciplinary programs adopted across the United States and in several foreign nations.

John Driscoll teaches economics and government in the Fairfax County, Virginia, Public Schools. He is a member of the NCSS Advisory Committee on Instructional Media and Technology. He has served as consultant to the Junior Achievement Applied Economics Program and has written for the *Washington Post.*

Elizabeth Dudley teaches at the Cambridge Friends School in Cambridge, Massachusetts. She has taught 7th and 8th grade English and social studies for eight years. During 1987–1988, she took a leave of absence to travel, write, and spend time on her farm in Idaho.

Pauline U. Dyson, a history–social studies teacher and department chair at Coginchaug Regional High School in Durham, Connecticut, is an NEH Resident Teaching Fellow of Western Civilization at the University of Connecticut. She has written on social history and role-playing for *Social Education* and *Teaching History.*

Michael Huff teaches social studies at Mendham High School in New Jersey. His undergraduate degree is in social studies education and he has a master's degree in international relations.

Lise Melancon is a 1st and 2d grade teacher at Indianola Informal Elementary School in Columbus, Ohio. She and her colleague Suzanne Peters have made presentations at the Great Lakes Regional Conference of NCSS and the Ohio Council of Social Studies Conference.

Kevin O'Reilly, who teaches at the Hamilton-Wenham Regional High School in Massachusetts, was the 1986 NCSS–*Time Magazine* National Outstanding Social Studies Teacher. He is the author of the four-volume series, *Critical Thinking in American History*, and coauthor of *Critical Viewing: Stimulant to Critical Thinking.*

Stuart B. Palonsky is Associate Professor of Social Studies Education at the University of Missouri–Columbia. His book *900 Shows a Year* (1986) examines social studies teaching in a suburban high school.

Suzanne Peters teaches grades K–1 at the Indianola Informal Alternative School in Columbus, Ohio. She and Lise Melancon have won two Freedom Foundation Awards. She has also been honored as an outstanding cooperating teacher by Ohio State University and selected as one of Ohio's outstanding economics teachers.

Arthur D. Roberts is Professor of Education at the University of Connecticut. A former junior and senior high school social studies teacher, his primary work is in the field of curriculum development. He is a leader in the Association for Supervision and Curriculum Development at both the state and national levels and is coauthor of *Redefining General Education in the American High School* (1984).

Vincent Rogers is Professor of Education at the University of Connecticut. A former Fulbright Scholar at the University of London, he has been active in curriculum development projects in Kenya, Italy, Saudi Arabia, and Israel. He is a coauthor of the Ginn Social Studies Program and a past author of the Silver Burdett program. He is currently involved in a study of alternative means of assessing children's learning.

John Rossi is a teacher and chair of the Social Studies Department of El Cerrito High School in the San Francisco Bay Area. He served as president of the California Council for the Social Studies, 1977–1978, and as a member of the NCSS Board of Directors for three years.

Alice Seletsky is a teacher at Central Park East School in East Harlem in New York City. A teacher for nearly thirty years, she has published in *The Nation* and the *Elementary School Journal* and has coedited *Teachers Speak Out,* a collection of teacher-written or -narrated pieces.

Thomas P. Weinland is Professor of Curriculum and Instruction in the School of Education at the University of Connecticut. Previously a teacher and social studies department chair at Huntington High School in New York, he has written extensively on history, social studies, and museum education.

INTRODUCTION

How do teachers communicate with one another about their teaching and their classrooms? One answer to this question is an ironic "Very rarely; teachers are far too busy to talk about teaching." We can speculate that, since teaching is such a personal experience, many teachers are reluctant to discuss their work. Many of us confine discussion of our work to the description of the humorous and not-so-humorous incidents that crowd our day—a sort of latter-day *Up the Down Staircase* approach to describing our work. This bulletin brings together the writing of some very good teachers who have found both the courage and the time to describe what they are doing with young people in their classrooms.

Why this bulletin? Stated most simply, we wanted to acknowledge the best that we do as social studies teachers. By doing so, we hoped to provide a rich storehouse of ideas and activities from which others could freely borrow—adapting and applying these ideas to their own teaching. These ideas go well beyond the bag of tricks or list of teacher-proof methods. We hoped that readers would draw a deeper understanding from what and how these teachers *think* about teaching. Our purpose was not to add to the burgeoning literature on scope and sequence or to add yet another definition of social studies. We had no plans to initiate a new direction for the social studies. In a field that seems to pride itself on redirection, we prefer to cast a vote for reflection—for drawing inspiration from the good things we do—so that each of us may become better.

We began work on this bulletin with a sense that there was a great deal of quiet excellence in classrooms that ought to be exposed. We are all painfully aware that every blemish on the educational body receives the widest exposure. Why not a book on what teachers are doing right? What we have come to discover as we read the contributions to this bulletin is the absence of metaphor. Although teachers often use military metaphors to describe their work—'in the trenches' or 'in the field', for the most part, our contributors speak of classrooms as classrooms, teaching as teaching, and students as kids, learners, or students. As we struggled to find the best title or theme for our work, the absence of metaphor seemed somehow significant: our contributors seemed secure enough in their work and with their audiences that metaphors were not necessary.

Our preliminary vision of this bulletin was that it should draw on a wide range of teachers, from different grades and different social studies subjects, from different geographical areas and from different communities. To that end, we contacted a large number of colleagues around the country and asked for their recommendations. We sought teachers from various programs who might offer something to a variety of teachers regardless of where or what they teach. We did our best to avoid a predisposed philosophy in our search and selection. Honesty compels us, however to conclude that advocates of content coverage as such and rote memorization will find little to applaud in this work.

In other respects, we were successful. We have included teachers from sub-
urbia and the city and from Massachusetts to California. We have included
primary teachers and teachers of senior electives, teachers who use highly
structured worksheets, and those who employ a less formal classroom structure. With few exceptions, we have not observed their teaching except through
their words.

We asked each teacher to tell us something of his or her philosophical
approach to teaching social studies. We urged that they keep this section brief
and focus primarily on what they do. We asked that they concentrate on a unit
or some small segment of a course to allow readers a window into the classroom. Most of the chapters in this bulletin contain specific questions and brief
selections from classroom materials. A few include worksheets and samples of
student work. As editors, we have taken the liberty of deleting portions of the
original work and we have made additions where we thought clarity or emphasis was needed.

We have employed a somewhat random assignment of chapters in this
bulletin. Readers who wish to read only about upper-elementary grade social
studies may find our decision frustrating, although the table of contents and
the headings of chapters will offer reliable clues as to the grade or subject
taught. We chose a random assignment to illustrate our belief that we have
much to learn from one another in our work—that a teacher of 3d graders and
a teacher of 12th grade sociology have a great deal in common. We have reined
in our professorial urge to hold forth at great length on any and all subjects
and have confined our comments to a brief concluding chapter, which represents an attempt to summarize common themes raised in preceding chapters
and to raise broader questions for our readers. Although we have had the last
word, we have no illusion about its being the best word. There are many good
words in this bulletin, and they are distributed throughout its pages.

In her introduction to *The Greek Way,* Edith Hamilton makes note of a fact
we often forget: As we marvel at the achievements of the ancient Greeks, we
must remember that we have no way of knowing whether we have seen their
best work. So it is with this bulletin. We are confident that our contributors
represent excellence, but we have no way of knowing whether they are the
best. Indeed, we suspect that many other teachers could have written descriptions of their work as important and compelling as those included here. We
should be surprised—and very disappointed—if we were wrong. Perhaps it is
important to remember that the eleven teachers represented here speak for
many others besides themselves. This bulletin is more than a resource and more
than a sampling of good teaching and good thinking about teaching. We hope
it will stand as a celebration of the best in each of us.

Vincent Rogers
Arthur D. Roberts
Thomas P. Weinland

CHAPTER 1

FOLLOWING OUR FOREBEARS' FOOTSTEPS:
FROM EXPEDITION TO UNDERSTANDING

Caroline S. Donnan

In the Beginning: A Vision in Vain?

I'm not sure whether the repetition was consciously planned or merely the result of circumstance, but somehow every even-numbered year they took us to the Columbus Zoo; on the odd-numbered years, we pushed display buttons at the Center for Science and Industry. Either way, the end-of-the-year field trip came and went each June with clockwork-like predictability. I remember, in December of my 5th grade year, my friend Jerry Confer told the class exactly where we'd be going six months before Mrs. Fallon ever did.

Don't misunderstand me. I liked the zoo and the science exhibits as much as any kid. I'm just not sure what they had to do with anything we'd ever done in class. I do recall that we couldn't wait for the bus rides back and forth. And I know these were about the only times any of us left the school grounds from one year to the next.

When I reached college age, a researcher came to speak to our student-teaching seminar. Rightly or wrongly, he said, the majority of new teachers would end up teaching in much the same manner that each had been taught. Whatever else his statement may have suggested, the image was vivid: There we were with one week left, Mrs. Fallon leading a full load of us all set to see action . . . and there we went, from reptile houses with snakes that never moved, to polar bears planted on pink blobs of paved bubble gum. I couldn't help but wonder if my students were doomed to have the same done to them.

Reworking the Curriculum: No Guts, No Glory

I was lucky. My first year of teaching was saved by three wonderful circumstances. First, I was far too busy keeping my head above water to learn how to get to the nearest zoo. Second, North Andover, Massachusetts, the town in which our classroom was located dated back to the early 1640s. Finally, I was new and possessed both blind faith and an untempered reserve of courage.

Mixed in somewhere was a healthy distaste for last-gasp field trips saved till June.

But where to begin? I looked around for raw resources—anything that might free my students and me from the schedule my own teachers had always seemed to hold so dear. Knowing nothing specifically of local history but convinced that, since we all lived in a small New England town, we must be sitting right in the middle of something, I was off and running. In my pocket, I always kept a supply of file cards to scribble down any excuse I could think of for a class expedition.

I also searched for engaging questions and tales of everyday life. Together they served as a catalyst for our activities and provided a common thread to help lead us from one exploration to the next. My role, then, was as class storyteller, researching and collecting memorable quips and bits of knowledge, combining them into a yearlong, real-life narrative told in installments each noon as 25 of us sat in a circle. From the first day, each of my 3d grade students adopted the family name of an original settler and thereafter assumed those settlers' names and historical roles in everything we did.

I used mornings for subject areas that required the classroom setting. I needed that time, too, to ensure myself solid standing in the eyes of parents who looked for familiar 3d grade seatwork each day in their children's bookbags and who might not understand the value of our expeditions until later in the year. Afternoons, though, were reserved for going out into the field to poke around backyards, crawl into cellar holes, pore over gravestones, or discover hideouts for the Underground Railroad. Very quickly it became precious time to all of us, and we guarded that time zealously.

In due course, we reenacted our way in and out of a full-day sabbath (Sunday) in the oldest meetinghouse, a kidnapping by Indians near the town whipping post, six town meetings in original taverns and inns, a roof fire, the rules of colonial etiquette from school desk to dinner table, a day in the haunted Loring homestead, ciphering on slates under the tutelage of "Old Put," and, among other things, a trial from the actual court records of Sarah Carrier's witchcraft indictment.

When we couldn't get to real locations, we worked on constructing our own original one-room "town founder's house" (located at one end of the classroom) or practiced scenes that eventually became "Starting from Scratch," a full-length musical relating the town's earliest history. We also spent a substantial amount of time writing settler diaries, field notes, notices for the meetinghouse, town records, sermons, poems, trip lists, hymns, project progress reports, hypotheses, and conclusions. And we drew maps and charts, costumes and scenery, fences and rooftops.

By the end of the year, 7th graders and high school seniors, required to pass a course covering the town's history, came to learn from us. The 3d graders led them on several explorations, but one of the most memorable was architectural. "See that roof and see how it has more on it than that one?" Courtney began. "Why do you think they did that—the extra, I mean?" Pitched roof led to saltbox and saltbox to hip, then on to gambrel, and eventually mansard. Each roof had a reason for being, explained Courtney and several other voices around her. So did each floor plan, each chimney shape and placement, each fence type, each gravestone and the symbolic art on it. As eight-year-olds ran down three-hundred-year-old roads to point out their discoveries, learning that had once been tentative took the form of a much more confident "Don't you see?" Each of our original questions, posed as catalysts for afternoon expeditions, had come full circle as students helped others join in their process.

All along the way, whether on a shared exploration, through settler diaries, or in their class musical, each colonist was always sure to point out his or her family's role in each episode. Rather than learning about history, they became that history, and all made sure they wouldn't be forgotten. Most of all, our afternoons were alive with that wonderful excitement that comes from personally digging in and doing. There clearly wasn't enough space in the classroom as we explored, discovered, verified, and authenticated three hundred years of the human adventure.

We had but one problem. In all the pages of the neatly typed, carefully bound, district-required social studies curriculum, never once was there mention of any of this.

"Doing" the Curriculum: Patterns and Processes in Action

For accountability's sake, I kept an ongoing checklist. Early in the year, for instance, as we sat on our knees interpreting the original house-lot plan for the town, students began to get a sense of North, South, East, and West. Allison addressed the others, "I'm thinking of a place east of the river, way south of the common, and to the west from Goody Foster's land." Nathan walked his fingers from Allison's lot to that of Goodman Farnum. I took the page I'd copied from the social studies teacher's edition and put a temporary check beside "Directions." Several days later we drew large squares over the plan and superimposed a topographical map of the area. By Friday, teams of three settlers used familiar landforms to find their actual homesites out in the field. I soon knew I could mark off "Map Skills" with confidence. The checklist, now tucked in the back of my file box, was a reference point for studies that naturally unfolded around us.

When Krissy asked why so many of the lots were on a hill, but some definitely weren't, we had ample reason to cover "Economic Principles," "Community," and eventually "Government." Later in the year we explored a family's chimney with seats built on the inside of each wall and on one outing Jamie found one of "his" family gravestones bearing news that he had "departed this life . . . being melted to death by extreme heat." Even "Climate" fell into place.

It would have been easy to become swept up in our growing enthusiasm. So, from time to time, I went back to that original checklist, reviewing its contents, and reassessing how the district would say we were doing. My own goal was fairly simple: to substantiate clearly each of our field studies—to "toe the line," as the settlers would say—while taking time to dance along it, too.

Unraveling the town's history, then, became the common vehicle for covering many skill and subject areas. It was also a wonderful excuse to put students in the position of discoverers, gatherers, and inquirers.

To usher in each afternoon's activities, students collected materials and field notes from projects in progress, donned ancestral name cards, and gathered for the day's introduction. Our afternoon studies followed a general pattern that recurred throughout the year: (1) information and/or story, (2) key question, (3) planning, (4) exploration, (5) recording, (6) sharing, and (7) new questions, connections, information.

Usually a story formed the basis of each study, told aloud from my file card notes. A key question at the end (initiated either by a student or by me) served to introduce the accompanying exploration. I might, for example, ask the Reverend Francis Dane (3d grade Paul) to come sit beside me as I told how each of the minister's three wives died, how his third wife had been the only woman to have land in her own name, and how the Reverend had played a leading role in trying to stay the frenzy of witchcraft. Telling how his daughters and even the minister himself were eventually accused of witchcraft, I shifted the focus toward our trip to the Dane homestead: "As the Reverend Mr. Dane's neighbors and parishioners, be thinking what traces of evidence you might find that would lead you to suspect even him of witchcraft."

Typically, class planning sessions preceded field expeditions. During these, settlers began to speak up and protect what they believed were their individual roles. Goodmen (that is, Mr.) Osgood and Holt, for instance, knew they had laid out some of the first roads in town. They took the lead in plotting the route to the Reverend Mr. Dane's house. Goodmen Johnson (fence-viewer) and Lovejoy (surveyor of highways) checked which fields we could cut across along the way and Goodman Barker was by now familiar with every bridge in town, having planned them all originally. Meanwhile Goodman Parker (scrivener by trade) collected class clipboards, Samuel Blanchard (owner of the local paper mill) affixed record sheets, while Benjamin Woodbridge (teacher and first to graduate from Harvard) insisted on passing out pens. To claim a job during each expedition, students had to explain their families' qualifications according to the times.

Next came actual exploration in the field. For this particular trip, Goodmen Allen and Bridges (constables) were responsible for pulling up the rear as we walked to the site itself. John Osgood (head of the militia), on the other hand, led the way. Innkeepers Faulkner, Parker, and Great John Frye (all 300 pounds of him) manned the cooler (or in cold weather, the thermos), which was usually pulled in our class wagon by one of the Farnum family (wheelwrights for four generations).

As we approached the Dane house lot, we reviewed the day's key question and how we would keep records. Then, "What here might possibly look a bit witchy?" and the settlers were off to comb the premises. Their findings—sketches or words recorded in a boxlike grid—would become material for the next day's discussion.

"I think it has to do with forks. Reverend Dane had some. Did you see them? Remember in the Parson Barnard House they didn't have any at all? Just knives and spoons in that house. Why was there a fork in this house and not in that one? I think it looks like the thing a devil holds. You know, his pointy fork," reported one student. Goodman Ballard, the first to bring a witchcraft case against a citizen, would later use this information in our own witchcraft trial.

Finally, we would end the Dane expedition by tying it to the original story: "And when Goody Lovejoy finally saw him carrying the big, black kettle, she absolutely knew it had to be . . ." I filled in a bit of historical background for the frenzy, settlers wrote in diaries, and this trip soon became the stepping-stone to other stories, expeditions, and eventually the trial.

Thus, each of our many studies reconfirmed the basic pattern, moving from information or story to key question, then from careful planning to field exploration, and on to recording, sharing, and finally to new questions, connections, information. Beyond that format, the actual order of these field experiences became critical. Students were primed for the subtleties of a minister's being accused of witchcraft, for instance, because they had already fully explored and then reenacted the colonial sabbath day—from writing their own hymns, prayers, sermons, rules of conduct, and public notices to researching and recreating the noon-house meal, clothing, tithing rod discipline, the deaconing of hymns, seating plans, deaf pews, and ancestral responsibilities for that day.

"Minding" the Curriculum: From Process to Hypothesis

Far beyond the pure adventure of our expeditions, the sort of thinking that naturally evolved because of them was and is remarkable. One such time was the week Captain Dudley Bradstreet (Nicole) spent "dignifying the pews"—creating a seating plan for the meetinghouse according to social status. A disagreeable task in those days, this ranking was historically a source of deep jealousies and hard feelings. No one in our class could believe Nicole wouldn't love the job, though they had heard Bradstreet detested it. Nicole went from classmate to classmate, interviewing them about their work, their family, their possessions, property, and livestock. As she sorted and reordered her stack of note cards (one for each classmate), anxious settlers peeked over her shoulders, offered free labor for favors in return, dropped their previous complaints from the constables' agenda. Despite many simultaneous activities, the room began to revolve around Nicole. I could feel the pockets of resentment, the relief of do-gooders.

Diary time proved fruitful. I began, "Captain Dudley Bradstreet has been busy dignifying the pews for sabbath day. As a fellow citizen, how do you think he's doing?" Pencils scratched purposefully at paper notebooks.

"Not good. Once he sued me but it wasn't my horse that did the damage (a true incident). I bet I'll be put in the back." Another settler wrote, "He caught my husband with a hat in court. He was more or less right because it *is* the law to do that. So, he doesn't like me. I think Bradstreet is okay. George Abbott is making lots of cushions for the meetinghouse. He likes Bradstreet. I think I do, too. Probably." Some students wrote about where they thought Dudley would be in ten years: "He makes me mad. I surely would like to have his job today." The 3d grade was not surprised to hear in later stories that Bradstreet was at once one of the most respected citizens (called the "worshipful Mr.

Bradstreet") and then, soon after, an accused witch who was driven from his home and into hiding by fellow citizens.

Often our explorations focused directly on hypotheses. For instance, the first of numerous Burying Ground Expeditions centered on investigating a common belief: "People say settlers didn't live as long as we do these days. What can you find here to prove whether or not that is true?" The class spread out to inspect gravestones. Scribbled columns of notes later turned into graphs and charts, subtraction and regrouping, smallpox and diptheria, questions and conclusions. Justin ran back to check in: "I got a ton of kids dead! I think you're right. I think they died not very old." Not everyone in the class was ready for higher-level thinking.

"But those were only some of them. And we got 46 more grown-ups than kids," reported Jonathan.

Now we were getting there. I asked the group collected on the grass, "Why did the children die?" Once again the troops scattered to re-search the burying ground.

"I think the kids got sick," offered Darren. Eventually the class discovered that sickness was rarely listed on "grown-up gravestones" but was specifically mentioned on the headstones of many children. Putting that together with a tally of how many people died at what ages, we came full circle to questions, connections, information. In point of fact, if settlers survived the first five years of life, their chances for survival were the same as they are today.

History provided a wealth of these questions ripe for exploration. One of my favorites was from the Johnson Cottage Expedition: "If ceilings were lower and beds not nearly so long, were people shorter back then?" But that's another episode . . .

Often we began these inquiries with an initial vote on the questions at hand. As in colonial days, use of a bean signified a negative response and a kernel of corn a positive one. We repeated the process again after our investigations had been completed. Almost always, this encouraged further analytical thinking, both individually and as a class. Over and over again discussions began with, "You changed your vote. What made you decide to do that?" Eventually we made a big poster to hang from the overhead heating pipes in our classroom: "Have a reason for what you believe" became an expected standard for class discussion.

In addition, a long time line stretched under a window sill that spanned one side of our room. I had to remember that eight-year-olds who fumbled with the concept of a month did not always move with total ease or comprehension from one century to the next. This time line prompted new awakenings and some funny discussions. Completely oriented to everyday inventions, it helped students put our trips in proper context.

A case in point, our Trunks and Trappings Expedition began with a visit to the local historical society. Karen wrinkled up her nose as she examined old clothing from one of the collections. "It's not really that nice," she commented. Upon checking her observation against the time line, we talked about the ramifications of life 100 years before scissors, 250 years before the zipper, and 280 years before any safety pins made it to America. That was not history as

INVENTIONS TIME LINE

1642	cast-iron stove		1839	bicycle
1676	screwdriver		1840	stamps
1683	12-inch ruler		1850	crayons
1690	bicycle (no pedals)		1860	washing machine
1693	wallpaper (England)		1864	window shades
1704	newspaper editions		1865	dynamite (Sweden)
1709	piano (Italy)		1867	barbed wire
1739	glass-making company (America)		1870	ice cream factory (England)
1750	umbrella (England)		1873	typewriter
1755	mirrors a luxury		1876	telephone
1755	drinking glasses a luxury		1877	record player
1760	pencil factory (Germany)		1880	car
1761	scissors now common		1880	lightbulb
1771	razors (France)		1880	breakfast cereal
1775	toilet		1884	fountain pen
1778	locks and keys		1885	can opener
1796	vaccination		1895	movies (France)
1799	anaesthetics		1895	radio (Italy)
1800	battery (Italy)		1899	tape recorder (France)
1805	push lawn mower		1899	aspirin
1807	street lights (England)		1901	vacuum cleaner
1807	steamship		1904	ice cream cone
1816	fire extinguisher		1905	airplane
1820	rubber band		1913	zipper
1824	cement		1914	traffic lights
1827	camera (France)		1918	women could vote
1830	sewing machine		1926	television
1830	railroads (England)		1932	parking meter
1832	streetcar (New York)		1935	hearing aids
1834	matches		1938	ballpoint pen
1834	refrigerator		1940	safety pin
1837	telegraph			

we normally think of it, but it made us pause, think, and look again a little more closely.

Undergirding the Curriculum: Logistics for Success

In addition to our patterned format, field experiences suggested specific procedures and equipment as well. Since all our trips were on foot, there were several key ingredients that were important to their success. The first was our tried and true little red wagon. We kept two in the classroom and took them on every outing. They were perfect for carrying emergency supplies, drinks, magnifying glasses, shovels, blankets, or even a settler with blisters. Wagon duty was always a favorite job.

Second, I always carried a whistle. Once we had gotten to a site and I had laid out boundaries, I believed in letting the students scatter in pairs to do their research. One long blast on the whistle meant "freeze wherever you are and listen for an update"; two short chirps meant "finish up and head to 'the hearth.'" (Since the hearth was the center of every colonial home, it became our trade name for a common meeting place.)

Third, clear expectations for behavior were critical. I arranged for one parent or student teacher to be on tap during every outing, who served one primary function: to provide a fast and firm trip back to school for students who exceeded two behavior warnings. The review of guidelines before we left, my whistle, and a raised hand signal usually did the trick.

As we walked along, students chatted with one another. But the rule was that when I raised my hand and stopped, talking stopped too. Our first two class trips literally consisted of merely practicing how to go down the road, stop, get instructions, and move on again. We had similar practice sessions with the one- and two-whistle routines, scattering and recollecting. This was a little embarrassing as passersby slowed and stared at our antics. If at first I felt uncomfortable with such a public regimen, within a week I knew it was a key factor in differentiating our expeditions from the wild and woolly recesses back at school. Mothers relaxed as we crossed busy streets. I relaxed as we crossed neighborhood lawns. Together we had an easy, orderly way to communicate and then get on with both the business and the excitement at hand.

Fourth, we named each expedition. With a common method for pinpointing which set of experiences we were talking about, we could easily refer to past history as well as past learnings.

Since nearly every trip involved some form of record keeping, 11-by-14-inch pieces of hard cardboard were a fifth key ingredient. These made inexpensive and indispensable clipboards. Before each exploration, recording sheets were taped to the boards, preventing the papers from coming unclipped or from blowing away. An additional sheet was always the bottom layer. It gave us the flexibility to change recording procedures or to do impromptu writing. Allowing several extra inches at the bottom of each board gave students room to rest their hands comfortably as their writing approached the end of a page. All clipboards came with settler names on them from the beginning, so those who couldn't resist poking pencil holes through them eventually lived with their own destruction.

Every student also had a felt-tip pen that was clipped onto a large yarn loop. These were worn around their necks each time we left school grounds. The felt tips alleviated both the problem of broken pencil points and the aggravation of ballpoint pens that won't write upside down. By indoctrinating students to hold the plastic top with one hand and pull the pen from it with the other, tops always stayed clipped onto the yarn and were seldom lost. This also left students' hands and pockets free whenever they weren't actually recording observations.

Finally, file cards and name cards were almost always with us. The settler name cards were wonderful tools for making our daily transition to another place and time in history. Printed in large letters and coated in clear contact paper, they were durable as well as helpful in calling one another by our historic names. In addition, I kept a continual supply of 3-by-5-inch file cards in my pocket. As I collected stories, they were easy to rearrange; new facts and anecdotes were integrated with old ones or set aside for special attention. In the field, follow-up questions, observations about a given child, ideas for future projects, quotes from excited settlers, or reminders of the day's objectives were easily scribbled and then filed for later use.

Realizing the Curriculum: A Cross-Check with Reality

Our study contained several inherent elements that deserve mention. Throughout our many field experiences, not every child was perfect. Certainly the spell was broken the day Beth Nelson's Irish setter followed us along the side of Old Academy Road and tipped over a neighbor's rabbit hutch. But a continual emphasis on record keeping, writing, reasoning, and accountability cleared potential fears from parents or from the administration and got us through the times when other people thought I was whistling in the dark. We had a definite purpose in being where we were, doing what we did, and everyone understood our assignment was to come back with material for future learning. That, in and of itself, made all the difference.

Another critical element in our study was the students' enthusiasm. From the outset, I wanted to involve the class by *digging in and doing*. The point was to do more than dress up like Thanksgiving Pilgrims, eat cranberry sauce off paper plates, and talk to Indians sporting crayola feathers. I wanted students to see differently the places they walked by every day and explore actively some of the things that make people tick. I wanted them to think. And I hoped they would feel the meaningfulness of their learning as well as the more obvious excitement of discovery.

Originally, I thought our backyard history would span about a month—better too short than too long. Instead, it grew and grew. At the end of an entire year we still searched for extra days and moments. Both our work on the "founder's house" and on the musical came into being when we looked for ways to extend our trips and bring the class's excitement inside. It would be dishonest to pretend either occurred without a great deal of borrowed time and more than a few after-school permission slips. On the other hand, it never occurred to any of us to stand in the way of honest momentum.

In Retrospect: A Vision Revitalized

Every once in a while, I think back to student teaching, to that college researcher and his grim prediction. More often, though, I wonder what my own elementary schoolmates would think of this present 3d grade class. I am not sure whether they would agree that I teach in the manner all of us had once been taught. Certainly they would see traces, for I doubt whether I am a negative instance for every statistic. But I should be proud if they said that at least these 3d grade settlers had a chance to learn in ways that many students learn best:

- by exploring, reexploring, and exploring a little harder
- by asking, listening, and writing
- by recording, comparing, connecting, and thinking always of another way of seeing
- and, most of all, by doing

Now, if I needed to, I suppose I could create some extra time to get my class to the nearest zoo. It is possible that our town may even have a center for science and industry close by. I think, however, that our explorations have reaffirmed something very important in my teaching and in my students' lives as well—something my 5th grade friend, Jerry Confer, probably knew all along. With all there is to learn and do in the outside world, we really shouldn't wait around until June to get started.

CHAPTER 2

MY NAME IS ALICE:

A FIFTH GRADE STORY OF NAMING AND FAMILY HISTORY

Alice Seletsky

My mother and father wanted my name to be part of their names. Their names were Neil and Diane. Since I was part of both of them, they wanted my name to be part of theirs. So they named me Nydia.

There are moments just before the start of school when I wish the children didn't have to show up. The room is ready, with everything perfectly in place. The red rug in the reading area has been shampooed and the striped cushion covers washed. The art area glistens with new paint brushes, unopened jars of paint, whole crayons, and 12 sharp scissors in the rack. Everything in the science area is folded, wound, packed, or boxed and neatly labeled. The book cabinets are freshly painted, and every book is in its proper place. The contact paper that covers some of the scarred table tops is smooth and unmarked. On the walls around the room, children's work is neatly mounted and artfully displayed. Who needs children in all this pristine splendor?

I feel that way about curriculum, too. I spend many hours of preparation, thinking up things for children to learn and do. I gather books, maps, pictures, and filmstrips. I make charts, lists, and video copies of interesting TV programs. I arrange museum visits and invite guest speakers. And along come the children, all 30 or 32 of them, with their own ideas, separate interests, and unique styles of thinking and working. The path of learning, mine as well as theirs, grows rocky. There are all kinds of unexpected bumps and ruts. We turn a corner and a whole new vista opens up. Some kids are leaping ahead; some are lagging, not getting it. There are times when everyone needs me and times when no one does. Like the classroom, which all too soon gets that lived-in look, the curriculum, too, takes on the character of the children who are refashioning it, with my support, into learning that grows out of and illuminates their lived experience. They are forming knowledge; that's what it's all about.

Children Refashion the Curriculum

The 5th and 6th graders I teach are a lively, energetic group. The differences among them in age, cultural and economic background, academic strengths, special interests, and talents reflect the diversity we aim for in all the classes in our school. Central Park East I, the primary school, and Central Park East Secondary School share a building in East Harlem, a predominantly Hispanic neighborhood in Manhattan. Central Park East is a *public,* alternative school. Students come to us from many parts of the city, as well as from the school neighborhood, ensuring a broad heterogeneity. We accept students on a first-come, first-served basis, and selection is limited only by our effort to have an integrated student body made up of children of diverse racial, social, and economic backgrounds.

The curricula I write are intended for eleven- and twelve-year-olds, though the actual age range is wider than that since there are always a few younger children and others who are older because they have repeated a year. Many students know one another because our school is fairly small, and I come to know them well because they are with me for two years. Nevertheless, September begins with children who need to become a group, and a class that needs to become a community.

I like to begin the school year with a curriculum about names and naming and family histories. (On alternate years, I do autobiographies.) A colleague suggests that I call it a study rather than a curriculum, since it doesn't seem to have quite the weightiness and solemnity of a traditional curriculum. As a matter of fact, I intend it to be fun, though I hesitate to use the word 'fun' in the present climate of sober, no-frills education. Like others, I've been caught up in the spirit of the times and have to remind myself that "playing around" with ideas is every bit as important as facts and dates. So for the first eight weeks of school, we learn about what names mean to families, individuals, and whole societies through a curriculum that offers many points of access, many opportunities for children to share ideas and information, and that involves parents in the process of helping children form knowledge.

Students work on a variety of projects, in different media, and every child contributes to a collection of autobiographical pieces on how he/she came to have a particular name. These are typed, illustrated, duplicated, and shared with families and other classes in our school.

"Before I was born," Crystal wrote, "my mother's favorite singer was Crystal Gayle. So she said she would name her last child Crystal. When she looked it up in the name book, it meant 'bright and brilliant,' and that's just the kind of child she wanted. And that's what she got."

A little glitter and razzmatazz go a long way with children. I want them to be captivated from the moment they walk into the room. Clearly, the "schoolroom monastic" style of interior decoration that prevails in so many classrooms' drab walls, scarred furniture, the obligatory map or two, the notices about fire drills and school schedules won't do it. I'm inviting children to a feast of learning, and the room needs to declare itself as the place where it's all going to happen.

In some conspicuous place, often hanging from the overhead light fixtures, are the words 'What's in a Name?' in bright, bold, colorful letters. Equally conspicuous are names written on charts, displayed on walls: names of everyone in the class; ordinary names and unusual ones; names of historical figures, rock stars, favorite characters in books or films; names written in Armenian, Greek, and Hebrew alphabets, and some in Cyrillic and Chinese characters cut from newspapers. There are signs which say "If Sandwich didn't invent the sandwich, who did?" or "What do Una, Primo, and Ichiko have in common?" Displayed on the interest table and in other parts of the room are writings and art work produced by students who have done this curriculum in earlier years and a variety of trade books about names and naming.

We start with a conversation about all this. Are any of the alphabets recognizable? Any of the names? Are there important ones I've left out? Why are names important? Why are we going to be learning about them?

Family History

Family history is going to be part of the study, and we talk about what it is and how we're going to do it. To wind up the session, I read aloud from William Saroyan's *My Name Is Aram*. (Hearing stories read aloud and talking about them together is an especially important part of the shared experiences of the classroom, and I read to the children for about half an hour every day throughout the year.) Saroyan's book is a warm and funny evocation of childhood within a family that, in addition to its other marvelous qualities, has a wonderful collection of names. The fact that I'm Armenian, as Saroyan is, contributes another dimension to the reading. It gives me the opportunity to link some of my own family stories to his and add the spoken and written language as still another component. It makes it possible for some children to think about the importance of a family's native language and the role it plays in family life.

"My middle name is Yuvia (Lluvia)," wrote Mayra. "It means 'rain' in Spanish. Here is the story of how I got it. It was early May, and Texas was having a severe drought. The whole state was dry. Then all of a sudden, it started to rain. That's when I was born. Everyone who was indoors ran outside and started dancing. My mom thought it was good luck, so she named me Yuvia."

And, thinking of unusual names, David wrote, "My father wanted to name me after my mother's father, Hermengildo, and after his own father, Marcelo. My name would have been Hermengildo Marcelo. Wow!"

Why names? Because they are places of beginnings and origins, and ways to establish a common ground for everyone in the group. There are large clusters of ideas that I want children to explore, which go beyond the stories of their own names. What happens, for example, when one's name is taken away—the humiliation and dehumanization of concentration camps and prisons where numbers are substituted for names; how immigrants felt when they were given other names because their own were too difficult to pronounce; how children felt when they were told their family names had been changed.

"My family's original name was Schwartzright," Matt wrote, "but my grandpa and gramdma changed it to Sherwin because Schwartzright is a Jewish name. At that time, Jews could not get work because people would tell them 'No Jews allowed.' They changed it to Sherwin, an English name, so they could get jobs."

We also discussed what happens when colonizing powers choose names for subjugated peoples, and how names and nationhood are reclaimed together at the time of independence. Another aspect of the topic is the history and development of language, since words are the names of things, and the roots of spoken language are evident in the process of naming.

Exploring the Third World

I'm not suggesting that we cover all these topics in the course of our studies, but I need to keep such a range of subjects in mind when I plan because I'm never quite sure what direction the discussions will take, and where the children's interests will lead. Some years ago, a small group of students became interested in the names of newly independent countries of the third world. They began to explore the topic, and their enthusiasm was so contagious that many children followed their lead in comparing old maps and atlases with new ones, writing letters to embassies and UN missions, gathering information about how and why the new names were chosen.

Three or four times a week, we arrange the chairs in a circle and have a discussion about topics like these. The questions I raise are open-ended ones— What do you think was the very, very *first* name? Or, why do so many kids have the nickname 'Papo'? What I'm after here is speculation and hypothesizing, *what ifs* and *how comes*—playing around with ideas. The facts and dates, the specific information about theories of language formation, for example, naming rituals in primal societies, or social and cultural patterns of naming in various parts of the world will come later, usually in the form of short lectures that I deliver. I'm not especially knowledgeable about linguistics or philology, but the story of languages fascinates me. I tell it as well as I can, using my carefully prepared notes. I share those notes with the children sometimes and describe how I prepare them. I want them to know that knowledge isn't just there in my head, ready to pop out; I have to work at putting ideas together, just as they do.

I often use a process called reflection. I offer a word or an idea, and each student has to say one or two things about it, trying not to repeat what someone else has said. I make notes and summarize, restating what has been said and adding my own comments. (The process was developed by Patricia Carini and the staff of the Prospect Center for Education and Research in North Bennington, Vermont. It was not originally intended for use with children, but I have found it works very well.)

The following excerpts from my journal give the flavor of some of those conversations with my students:

Everything has to have a name, otherwise people would just be making noises to each other, and nobody would know what the noises meant. Every word is a name. Every word is the name of something, except words like 'the', 'and', 'it', and 'this'. Jahmal disagreed and said people use the word "this" instead of pointing, so it is the name of a gesture. Some people think every single word has a meaning, including every name. Others think some words and names are just sounds and don't mean anything. I said that in some languages, a certain kind of sound, "tsk," for example, has a special meaning, but only for people who know that language.

We talked about names that are family traditions. You get named after somebody in your family who is dead, and it's supposed to make you remember that person. But it doesn't always happen that way. Izzy says he's not sure his mother is thinking about his grandfather, who is dead, every time she says Izzy's name. Some people don't like their names, so they take a nickname. Or a baby brother or sister can start mispronouncing your name, and that can become your nickname.

The topic for another conversation was surnames—very common like Smith, Jones, Rivera, and more unusual ones like Bryszienski and Sriskandarajah. I read excerpts from Milton Meltzer's *A Book about Names* including the problems they had in China where 4800 women in a single district had exactly the same name. This led to interest in the number of Smiths and Joneses in New York. Children used telephone directories to gather data on numbers and types of names. We began to identify certain name endings like *-sky, -ian, -son,* and *-ette* as having particular national origins. We investigated the meanings of 'Van', 'Von', or 'De' and discussed the practice of hyphenating names. I gave many different homework assignments having to do with names in the phone book: the longest and the shortest, the one with the greatest number of consonants or vowels, names that name objects like Bean and Stone, names that name colors, names that describe work, and so on. I recorded one of these discussions in my journal:

Jamella came in with another funny name from the phone book: Goldie Fish. I told my story about the Lear family who named their daughters Chanda and Gonda and a millionaire named Gogg who named his daughters Ima and Yura. We talked about the kinds of names that never appear as surnames like Dog, Cat, Elephant— although somebody had Oliphant and said it was the same thing. Ashanti pointed out that some of those names are used among Native Americans and other tribal people; 'Black Elk' was the example he gave. Other children came up with other examples. Finally, someone brought up 'Roach' and refused to believe me when I pointed out that it was a perfectly good Anglo-Saxon name. Why would anybody use such a name, they asked; who would want to be called Roach? And are there any roaches in England? I said I'd look up the origins in the OED and report back.

The telephone directories were getting a workout, and I found myself giving a number of impromptu lessons on various aspects of alphabetizing. It appeared to be one of those skills which many kids had "learned," to the extent that they could put half a dozen words in alphabetical order if they had to, but they couldn't actually use the knowledge they had to locate particular names in the directory with any ease. As the children continued to compile lists, they began to identify many surnames of European origin, and began using Spanish, French, German, and Italian dictionaries to confirm guesses and check on meanings.

Active learning can't take place unless the classroom is arranged in ways that support children's choices and activities. In my room, work areas are designated and appropriately provisioned: art, clay, cooking, a reading corner with lots of books, science, math, computer, dress-up. Maps, globes, atlases, history books, and encyclopedias are in a special reference corner. For the past two years, I've had the use of an unused room adjacent to mine, and we've been able to spread out. Before that, I had an ordinary classroom of average size. All of it is just as do-able in one room as in two; the latter is just so much more comfortable. One corner of the room, walled by two book cabinets, is my private domain. A beautifully lettered sign, arching over the narrow opening, announces it as "Elysian Fields." Before the year is out, most of the children come to know that it was the place where the dead heroes of Greek mythology ended up.

The projects that children work on are often, but not always, related to the curriculum theme. (Art for its own sake is every bit as important as art in the service of some other kind of learning.) Children work at mapmaking and model building, murals, sculpture, pottery, stitchery, illustrated books and written reports, board games, computer activities, graphs, charts, dioramas, improvised drama, reading—and anything else that seems appropriate. I regard these as an essential part of each day's work and expect children to take them seriously. In all the formal and informal evaluations that I make of children during the course of the year, I include some analysis and description of this work.

As the study of names got under way, children worked on sculpting their own names in clay in a variety of designs, and some enterprising youngsters found bread dough to be the medium of choice and baked their names. In the sewing area, needlepoint and soft-sculpture were the media: names were worked into colorful designs on plastic mesh, or embroidered on fabric, then padded to stand out in relief. Another favorite was name pillows: fabric cut in the shape of individual alphabet letters, stitched and stuffed to form the name of the maker. Print-making was another medium that children used, making mono-prints and colorgraphs of designs based on the letters and configurations of their names.

An activity that eventually included every child and resulted in a magnificent wall display was begun by the art teacher. She talked about flags and banners as another kind of symbolic name and helped children plan personal flags whose iconography was based on things important or special in each child's life. The completed pieces, done in water colors, oil, crayon, and felt marker were impressive because each so clearly reflected a particular child and, put side by side, gave a wonderfully fresh view of the whole group.

At our school, polls and surveys of various kinds of activities begin in the earliest grades. Small persons with clipboards appear from time to time, asking for permission to determine our preferences for particular colors, or animals, or flavors of ice cream; or we are asked to guess how many babies the hamsters will have this time around. The surveys that my 5th and 6th graders conducted in the course of this study of names were an extension of those early experiences in data collection. Using class registers, we tabulated the popularity of particular names and tried to make some influences about cultural or national origins of the names—Latino, African, French, German, or others. Children interviewed friends in other classes about preferences, nicknames, and names that had special meanings for families.

Once the data were gathered, they had to be put in some kind of order to make sense of our findings. This became a laborious process, involving much shuffling of papers and making tally marks. It would have been a perfect way to use the computer as a research tool. Computer literacy is not my strong suit. Neither is statistical analysis, but we got through it eventually, and the results, presented in the form of large charts, tables, pictographs, and bar graphs, all in living color, were wonderful to behold. Some of the children could describe the findings in written narrative form, but it was difficult for many others, including some who were reasonably fluent writers and speakers.

In my original plans, all these data were to have been combined with the children's individual reports and stories of how they were named into a comprehensive document. Each child would use it as the basis of a hand-bound, illustrated, personal book. My grand plan, it turned out, was a bit too grand for my resources and those of the class. Recopying graphs and tables to a reduced size, writing explanatory paragraphs for them, getting art work together all of the right size and shape, were activities for which nobody seemed to have much enthusiasm. The best we could manage, at the end of the study, was a simple collection of their stories and reports, typed by me, duplicated and stapled together in the form of a booklet.

Since each child was required to write one, I allowed considerable latitude in the scope and subject matter to be included in these reports. There was a broad range in ability among the children: some could write only the simplest kind of personal narrative, while others were ready for the more complex tasks of paraphrasing and interpreting information learned in interviews with parents and other family members, describing events and relationships, raising questions about tastes and preferences in naming. I wanted each contribution to represent the best that a particular child could do and for all the work to be equally valued by all the children.

We began with simple genealogical charts, lists of names and places of birth, names of siblings, and nicknames. Then children made similar charts for parents and grandparents after conducting interviews. Several wrote letters to grandparents or other family members who did not live nearby. Since parents were involved in helping children prepare the charts, bits and pieces of family history began to creep in: a child named after her mother's childhood friend; the objections of family members to particular names. "For the first two weeks of my life, my name was Jacob," Luke wrote. "My mom and dad loved the name Jacob, but everyone else in the family hated it, so they named me Lucas, after my great grandfather." Unusual names were noted, as well as places of origin. Using name labels and string, children transferred information about the birthplaces of parents and grandparents to large maps of the United States and the world. These were continually interesting to the kids, as more and more names were added. They consulted them a lot, talked about it among themselves, and were very clear in their explanations to visitors.

The interview questions we agreed on were such queries as the following: How did I get my name? Why did you choose it? Did anyone else in the family have suggestions? How did others react when you told them what my name was? Some children tape-recorded their interviews, others took notes, sometimes with the help of parents. Everyone wrote an official first draft in class, which I read carefully at home. I try not to write too many things on children's papers. I'm not sure many of them know how to interpret abbreviated comments or suggestions for changes. Instead I keep a detailed set of notes for myself and work with children individually on revisions of their work. For those who needed more time and attention than I was able to give, I enlisted the help of others—the special education teacher, our school librarian, school aides, and our student teacher. In some cases, I called home and asked parents to help, sharing my ideas and offering suggestions on how they might do it.

One of the reasons this study appeals to me so much is that it makes clear how we all have all sorts of common experiences that link us together. It is important for children to know that. As the stories and reports were written and shared, the common threads became clearer and clearer, so that children heard echoes of their stories in the stories of others.

"My mother picked Jahmal because she didn't want my name to be a European name. She wanted an African name. A couple of weeks before I was born, my mother and father went to a jazz concert. There was a jazz musician there called Ahmed Jahmal, and that's how I got my name."

Jamelah wrote on a similar theme: "My name is Arabic. My mother picked it out of an African book. I happen to like it a whole lot because it has that 'lah' in it, and it makes it sound sassy and musical. I like Johari [her middle name] too because it means jewel, and it makes me feel like a million bucks."

When the children read their work aloud to one another, there was another connection to Africa in Matthew's story that touched everyone:

> When my mom and dad went on their honeymoon to Africa, they went around with the Peace Corps, to see if they wanted to join. When they came to a village, whose name I can't pronounce, they met a boy about 11 whom they came to like very much. His name was Usman. One day, he asked my parents if he could come to America with them. Since his parents were dead, and he worked on his uncle's farm, "Why not?" thought my parents. So they asked the chief, and he said no, because Usman was owned by his uncles. A few years later, my parents were in a restaurant where they met the Peace Corps leader, and they asked him how Usman was doing. He said that Usman had died of malaria. So when I was born, they gave me his name.

Over the years, I have done a variety of studies with my students. I am in the enviable position of being relatively free to choose my own themes and develop them in ways I deem appropriate and interesting for the children I teach. I think of this as a privilege and cherish it all the more because it is threatened. Citywide social studies tests are being talked of, and one of these days they will happen.

The topics I have chosen range from family history to ancient history, and from a study of imaginary lands and utopias to the recent history of Southeast Asia. We do short units of study on current affairs that we reenact in the classroom. A few years ago, when we were fortunate enough to have Chinese pen pals, we learned about modern China. I also have old favorites, which I return to every few years. Ancient Greek civilization is one of these. I revise it each time I do it to make a better fit with the particular group of children, but it remains essentially a humanities course—an amalgam of history, geography, literature, with myth, folklore, social history, art, and architecture as strands of varying importance.

I make these choices because one of my responsibilities as an educator is to make decisions about what is worth knowing and help children recognize that there are things in the world to be valued. I want them to understand what valuing means, how to express itself in our society, and how it is tied to what was valued in the past. I would like children to recognize the remarkable inventiveness of human beings and to think about what has happened to the ideas and artifacts produced by human imagination and effort.

I don't worry much about relevance or motivation; I try to write curriculum that offers many different ways of getting at ideas and many levels on which children can engage with them. I look to see what has attracted and caught the attention of a child as well as groups of children. In my secret heart, I always hope that something will arouse a passion for the subject that matches mine; on the rare occasions when it happens, it is a thrill unlike any other.

I find it difficult to think of children, content, and classroom as separate elements. What I teach is inextricably bound up with who the youngsters are in a particular group, and how they operate as learners in the classroom. I cannot think of curriculum as an abstraction or as prescriptions, goals, strategies, and outcomes. Though my *ideal* curriculum is a thing of breathtaking originality and seamless construction that would be utterly fascinating to every single child, reality is a little different. I am clear about what I want children to think about and learn, but the form of the curriculum is fluid and untidy—bits and pieces dribble off the edges, and there are little gaps that don't get filled up. Some threads of ideas meander here and there, but don't get very far.

I am not as uncomfortable with this as I once was. The knowledge we form in our heads—adults and children alike—is not a seamless fabric in which ideas are woven together into a fixed pattern and held tightly in place. It is more a matter of pieces of knowledge, some understood fully, some less so but with clear links, and whole clusters of notions that rattle around, looking for a place to fit in. Some are useful, some interesting, some mistaken. Part of the learning process is to be conscious of all this, to figure out what the useful parts are and how they can fit together so we can make some sensible interpretations of the world. Though there are many commonalities, each child puts ideas together in a different way and thinks the world differently from his or her neighbor. One of my purposes as a teacher is to help make children aware of this, to give them the tools to articulate the "world-in-the-head" and share it with others.

CHAPTER 3

HONOR THE EARTH:

LEARNING FROM NATIVE AMERICANS*

Mari DeRoche

Everybody needs a rock. Tim needs his to hold and feel the smoothness when he is having trouble sitting still in reading group. Nicole likes looking at her piece of pink quartz that she keeps on her desk. It reminds her of being in Maine with her father. That's where she picked it up and it became hers. Alison keeps her rock in her pocket and likes to make up stories about what it tells her.

Tara has a friend that happens to be a tree. She leans on it in all the seasons and "watches it live." Rae carries around an acorn because she likes "the way it fits right into my hand." These rock and tree lovers are my 3d grade students.

Sometimes a rock goes clattering across a desk, just when I'm presenting a new math concept. Once a desk cubby fell over spilling leaves and acorns all over the just-vacuumed floor. The custodian was there, telling me that I must do something about the growing sugar crystals that were attracting ants on the back counter.

At these times, I reach for my own smooth, round stone and remind myself that classroom silence and tidiness are desirable, but not more important than having students bring nature into the classroom.

I believe our planet is in danger. Toxic and nuclear wastes contaminate our water, land, and air. People are warring in the Persian Gulf and on the Los Angeles highways. People are starving and homeless in Ethiopia and in Hartford, Connecticut. Nuclear weapons threaten the existence of all life.

I think we can become better caretakers of the Earth and of people. Teachers can influence what will happen in the world in the next few decades. We can—and must—make a positive difference. I hope that by helping students form personal connections with the beauty of the Earth, they will take responsibility for making it a better place to live. *Honor the Earth, Learning from Native Americans* is a curriculum that I have developed to help my 3d grade students form these connections.

Charter Oak Neighborhood School in West Hartford is where I teach and learn. In our K–6, four-hundred-students population, many languages are spoken. About 50 students requiring intensive special education for a variety

---

*"Honor the Earth" is a 1987 recipient of a Celebration of Excellence Award. This award is presented by the Connecticut State Department of Education and Southern New England Telephone.

of learning disabilities are mainstreamed into regular classrooms at Charter Oak. Seven of them are in the 3d grade.

My team partner Laura and I spent three months last year with our thirty 3d graders, honoring the Earth and learning about and from Native Americans. Our faithful and patient aide, Ann, helped us in every way—though she didn't honor bees and she didn't do snakes.

We started our immersion into Native American ways of life by forming cooperative learning groups that we called tribes.

Each of the five tribes had six members. We assigned each group the name of a real Native People who had lived or are now living in Connecticut (Pequot and Mohegan, for example). We talked about how people need to behave together so that everyone in the group is successful. The people of each tribe made a list and we took from each to form a class list. It included helping each other, encouraging, participating, taking responsibility for completing work, and considering the needs of others.

We wrote our new tribal names on the board with permanent chalk. We told the tribes that they would earn points for the positive tribal behavior shown on the list they had created. Each person in the tribe would receive a feather for every five points earned by his or her tribe. This "Native American behavior modification" plan worked like a charm. Feathers became more valued than stickers. They were also earned by individuals for excellent research, creative story writing, and acts of kindness and generosity.

We had dozens of books, illustrations, and filmstrips about Native Americans in centers around the room.

One center included filmstrips of New England Indians. Two students at a time viewed a film and created question and answer cards. Example: What foods were called the three sisters? Answer: corn, squash, and beans. The cards were placed on a bulletin board and tribes studied together in preparation for Jeopardy games.

The "Medicine Wheel Center"[1] was a reference chart of Sun Bears Earth Astrology. A student found his or her birthdate on the chart to discover personal symbols. Sparkling River (all students took Nature names) wrote, "I was born in the moon of the big winds. My special animal is a cougar and my plant is plantain. A special mineral to me is turquoise. I was born in the north where the white buffalo is the spirit keeper."

Other centers included rock, mineral, and shell collections with identification books. Books on birds, plants, and animals helped students to recognize symbols like flicker, blue callas, and marten. Identification coloring books were available to be copied and colored.

Making a wigwam village kept us busy for weeks. One foot was scaled to one inch. Little people were made from clothespins, cloth, and yarn. Wigwam frames of twigs and pipe cleaners were covered with birch bark. Clay was used for dugout canoes, pots, and mortar and pestles.

On the wall were maps of Connecticut, New England, the United States, and the world. Connecticut was outlined on each of the maps. As often as possible we referred to the maps so that students had a sense of where they were in the world *and* to show that Indians lived differently in different parts of the country.

The focus in this curriculum is on southern New England woodland people, but we compare and contrast by teaching briefly about other native people in North America. For example, we study the Cherokee and the Trail of Tears; how a great many of them were forced from their homes in the Great Smoky Mountains to live on a reservation in Oklahoma. We study the Buffalo Hunters in the central plains, the Village Dwellers in the Southwest, and the people of the northwest coast who created totem poles. *We emphasize constantly that the land and the climate and ancient traditions make these people different from each other. There is no stereotyped Indian.* Age and ability levels determine depth of study for the various groups.

Ecology is an important part of the project. We study about how plants, animals, the land, and people depend on each other for survival. We, the people, are the caretakers of Earth.

Native Americans had strong connections with Mother Earth before non-native people came. They never wasted her gifts and were always thankful for them. When Dutch traders came to the northeast shores of Turtle Island, they brought iron pots, blankets, and powerful "thunder sticks." The native people were fascinated and came to value and want these new things. They bought them with beaver skins, but soon most of the beaver had been killed.

The connection with Mother Earth was beginning to break. The native people realized what they had done, but it was too late. When thousands of them began to die from chicken pox, they believed that they were being punished by the Great Spirit. The men who carried chicken pox here from across the sea did not die, for they had built up immunities. The native people thought that these white men had been chosen by the Great Spirit to live on the land.

We learned that the native people's belief about being punished wasn't true. We also learned that by wasting the beaver the balance of nature was upset.

Each gift from Mother Earth and Father Sky possessed special qualities. The children seemed instinctively to know what they were. They said that the grizzly bear was very strong and powerful. He has great courage and is very wise. The deer is swift and beautiful. She provides food and clothing for people. The fawn is gentle and loving. The wolf knows how to get what she wants. She protects her babies and is a good hunter. The eagle is bright and flies high, seeing everything at once. He is a good leader. Some kids knew that the beaver is eager and works very hard.

In the classroom, each child adopted a "nature name." We asked children to think about what was special to them in the natural world. We talked about stones and crystals. Animals came next. We talked about all of the animals that live in southern New England: the four-legged, the winged, those that slither and crawl, and those that swim. We talked about gifts from Father Sky: the moon, the sun, stars, planets, and rainbows. We thought of the clouds, rain, thunder, and lightning.

Some of the students knew their nature names right away. Others needed more time to think. Some asked other students or adults for suggestions. Within a few days, Crystal Fire, Brave Wolf, Rainbow Spirit, Pretty Deer, Yellow Feather, and all the others were ready to start their journeys—journeys that would lead them to discover new places *inside themselves,* to explore our land in different ways, and to make personal connections with other living beings on the Earth.

We began our work with a trip to the American Archaeological Institute in Washington, Connecticut. It proved to be our *most* valuable resource for learning about how the woodland people lived.

The hour-long bus ride took us through the beautiful backwoods of Connecticut. We (the one-third of us who didn't get bus sick) imagined how it was when the native people lived there. Finally, at the museum, we were shown the inside of a longhouse. The kids got to grind corn, handle lacrosse sticks, blow a moose horn and examine raw hide, untanned and tanned deer skin, baskets, and clay pots. They learned about dugout and birchbark canoes. They were able to go inside the wigwams in the authentically reconstructed village.

While eating lunch outside, one of the kids discovered a snake. Within seconds, 25 others had descended upon it—some hesitantly but others with great vigor. They used sticks to try to pick it up. We had our first lesson of the wild *in* the wild. It was not easy. We sat down and talked about why it is important to respect animals and let them live peacefully in their natural habitats. We talked about endangered species and human greed. I hope we did not go overboard with guilt making.

Then we thought about how a Native American child would have treated the snake. We decided he would look the snake in the eye and say, "Hello, little brother. It's good to share this path with you on such a beautiful day." Then the snake and child would continue on their separate ways. (I hope the garter snake fully appreciated the absence of endangerment in its life. It was a close call. I wondered whether any students in the 3d grade class would ever wear snakeskin belts?)

Laura and I convinced our young naturists that research needed to be done if we were to learn about the Native Americans who lived here on Turtle Island (now North America) by the long Tidal River (Connecticut) before the new Americans came from across the sea. As a class we discussed the basic needs of all people and how the environment determined how those needs were met. Then we assigned research questions to each tribe. The Pequots were responsible for geographical facts, natural resources, climate, and weather. The Mohegans studied historical facts of southern New England, how the Native Americans came here from the Bering Strait, and learned about archaeology along the way. People in the Wampanoag Tribe covered food, shelter, and clothing. The Nipmunks took care of transportation, tools, and weapons. Language, government, and raising children were the Podunks' responsibility. The Paugussetts researched medicine and healing, ceremonies, sports, and games.

Members of each tribe worked together to prepare oral presentations. They were continually rewarded with feathers for encouragement of others, consideration, and participation. When each group was ready, they presented their information to the class.

Some members of each tribe were asked to write 20 to 30 questions and answers about their areas of research. Laura and I had to help a great deal with this task at the beginning. We added some of our own questions when important facts had been left out. Copies were made for each of the tribes and oral study groups were held to learn the information. We then had a great time playing Trivial Pursuit and Jeopardy games with the questions. With much of this factual background material in place, we were now ready to do more imaginative work.

When the students had looked at many pictures, filmstrips, and films about woodland villages, they were ready to start creating their own *imaginary* experiences in the native world. We introduced this activity through guided imagery. I explained that a good way to create a story is to let your mind show you the way. It was time to create a native family and this technique would help them imagine what theirs would be like. The first thing they needed to do was to lie on the floor on their backs, close their eyes, relax, and listen.

I began by reading to them in a soft, slow, quiet voice:

It's time to close your eyes and relax. Let your body sink into the floor and let yourself breathe smoothly and deeply. You are breathing in good clean air and energy and breathing out tension and worries. Relax the muscles in your face [pause] and your neck [pause]. Now feel your shoulders relaxing, your back, your arms. Your lower back is relaxing. Now your feet are feeling relaxed. You are feeling quiet, breathing smoothly.

As you are relaxing, let your mind wander to a beautiful forest. It is a warm sunny day, and you are walking near a stream in the forest. Look up and let your mind show you the trees, birds, and sky. Look on both sides of you. Are animals waiting there to be your friend? [Pause] After a while, you sit by a boulder to rest. You are dozing. When you look up, you see a wise person standing in front of you. Let your mind show you what this wise person is like. [Pause] This wise person gives you a gift. What is your gift? The wise person walks away.

It is time for you to return home. You walk back to your village. Notice what your village looks like and who is there. You walk back to your wigwams. Your family is there. Let your mind show you who lives there with you. You talk with your family, show them your gift.

Now it is time to come back to the room. You will go back to your village often in your mind. When you are ready, open your eyes. You will feel rested and alert. When you are ready, go back to your seat. It is time for you to share your experiences if you want to.

We had wonderful sharing. The "gifts" ranged from crystals to puppies, from rainbows to diamonds.

We used the guided-imagery technique many times. Sometimes we imagined what it would be like to live in an Indian family. We imagined ourselves as hunters, warriors, grandfathers, and babies.

After each guided-imagery session and sharing, we had quiet journal time. Students were encouraged to write about images and events they especially liked. They kept lists of new, special symbols. They were never assigned stories to write. They were told that, if they wrote a story, had it edited by an adult, copied it over carefully, and read it to the class, they would receive a red feather.

A red feather was the highest symbol of honor one could receive. We presented many red feathers. Here are some excerpts from their journals:

"My name is Crystal Fire. I was born eight summers ago in the year of the big flood . . ."

"My name is Brave Eagle. I live with my grandfather, Wise Owl. He teaches me to hunt and fish. I don't work in the garden. That is woman's work." [Of course, we discussed this very controversial idea!]

"Last night, my brother Strong Bear, and I were captured by our enemies, the Mohawks."

"I traveled with my uncle, Long Knife, to Plymouth. I had never seen a white person before. My uncle wanted to buy a powerful fire stick. My father says that the white ones will only bring us trouble. They come in their great canoes with wings to take our land. They do not know that we do not own the land. No man can own the land."

My Special Education students loved the story writing. Some of them were fine artists and collaborated with more able writers to create and illustrate their own books. We learned Indian Sign Language in our Special Education class. It is the most pleasant and effective way I have ever found to teach language arts skills. Robert Hofsinde's book, *Indian Sign Language*,[2] was our bible. Students learned sight vocabulary quickly by responding in sign to their flash cards. I would sign, *Man-Walk,* and they would write "A man is walking." Signing is a great way to help learning-disabled and non-English-speaking students learn about syntax. When they knew about 20 basic words, I signed to them and they would write the word I signed under noun, verb, or adjective. Signing stories to each other was also a popular activity. They signed, "I see a beautiful bird flying in the forest" and "The handsome man rode his horse into the forest."

Reluctantly, I introduced words like 'hunt', 'kill', and 'capture' into our signing vocabulary. The sentences were never quite the same after that. "The man killed the bird in the tree" just didn't seem comfortable to me, but the students saw nothing unusual about it. After all, they argued, the native people had to hunt to live. I became more realistic. After all, I do eat chicken and Big Macs.

Seven Arrows,[3] by Hyemeyohsts Storm, is about the Medicine Wheel of the Plains Indians. It is also about Indian shields. They were never intended to give protection in battle. Indian shields were too fragile. Sometimes they were made of buffalo, bear, or bull hides, but more often were covered with the soft skins of deer, antelope, coyote, otter, weasel, or even mice. They were hung with plumes, tassels, and pouches and painted with symbolic features. These things represented the individual Medicine and Clan Signs of the men who carried them. These signs told who the man was, what he sought to be, and what his loves, fears, and dreams were. Almost everything about him was reflected in the mirror of his shield.

Now it was time to make our own shields. The kids had been collecting pictures from *National Geographic* and other natural science magazines. Some had drawn their own. Each child carefully chose his or her most special symbols from the Earth, the water, and the skies. A local pizza man had generously donated a large pizza board for each person. For days, the students worked, meticulously stenciling their nature names and arranging each picture until it seemed to be in its right place. Finally it was time to add the feathers. They were glorious. Some encircled the shields. Some became parts of birds or rainbows. At the end, each shield truly reflected the dreams and personality of its maker.

Our unit on Native Americans was coming to an end. Our grand culmination was a presentation of our learning to the entire school assembly:

> Welcome, my name is Little Deer and this is Brave Snake. We have asked you to come here today to share our learning about Native Americans. Native Americans were the first people who lived on Turtle Island—the continent we now call North America. We will speak about the native people before and after the Europeans came to North America.

> Brave Snake: We have been learning about the culture of the Woodland People who lived right here in West Hartford and Hartford by the Connecticut River. Some of these people were called Mohegans and Pequots. We have also learned about the Plains People who lived very differently from the Woodland People.

> Little Deer: We are learning to see the Earth as the native people saw it—as a living being. We are learning to see the magic of all the Earth's children and the rocks, plants, animals, and the waters of Mother Earth.

> Brave Snake: We are learning about the magic of the clouds, sun, stars, the moon, and the rainbows of Father Sky.

> Little Deer: Red Hunter is here to tell us about how the first Native Americans came to Turtle Island—this continent we call North America.

Red Hunter tells how the people came to North America. He shows a big map of North America and tells how people came across Bering Strait and finally to New England.

> Brave Snake: Whenever we study a culture—how people live—we learn about how they get their food, clothing, and shelter. All people in the world need these things to live and survive.

Sunstreak reads a story of what the people eat and how they get their food. The children perform a corn dance. Rainbow Spirit tells about shelter. Yellow Feather tells about clothes. Sparkling River tells us about transportation.

> Little Deer: Woodland Indians in the Northeast mostly spoke the Algonquin language. We get words like 'chipmunk', 'squash', 'porcupine', and 'moccasin' from the Algonquins. Many of the tribes, however, had to use picture writing and hand sign language to understand each other. These are some examples of sign language.

The children demonstrated sign language and taught the audience to sign a few sentences. The presentation continued with music, dancing, a skit about the hunt and the ceremony in which the Indians thanked the deer for giving its life so that the people could live. They described the coming of the white man.

> When the Europeans started to come to the continent of North America, life changed in many important ways for the native people. Here are Wise Bear and Fast Deer to tell you how it happened.

Some of the great teachings of the Native Americans have been lost for a long time. The native people believed that the Earth was a wonderful gift from the Great Spirit and we must take responsibility for taking care of our planet.

For many years people came to North America and did not respect the Earth. They cut down trees that they did not need. They killed animals that they did not need. They polluted the air and the waters. They forgot to respect the Earth. They forgot to thank Mother Earth and Father Sky for all their gifts.

They killed many of the native people and took away their lands. New Americans and Native Americans had many battles and much sadness together.

Now new Americans like us from many countries are beginning to want to learn about the teachings of the Native Americans.

We want to end our program with a song by Molly Scott. It is called "We Are All One Planet." We will sing and sign this song in Indian sign language for you.

This song helped us learn about respecting our earth and each other. We are many new Americans from many different countries. We want to thank the Native Americans for our new learning.

We Are All One Planet

We are all one planet,
all one people of the earth.
All one planet, sharing our living
our dying, our birth,
and we won't stand by,
watching her die, hearing her cry and deny
We live as she lives,
We die as she dies.

So many ways to divide us,
so many ways to build boundaries and walls.
Systems we set up to hide us,
Neighborhoods, nations ignoring the call
of the beings who live outside of the boundaries
inside of the skins that are different from ours,
Creatures whose eyes, reflect the same skies,
and watch the same stars,
so many ways to hurt and not heal
to speak and not listen
to act and not feel
and too little time to be simple and see,
the circle includes every bird, every tree, every you, every me.

Think of the things we love.
Remember the ones we love.
Open our minds our hearts
and our hands.
And trust when we don't understand.

The curtain closed. First there was silence. Then applause. Then more applause. The audience loved our presentation. We learned about Native Americans, about nature and its relationship to people. We learned to imagine, to walk in other people's shoes. We learned something about commitment and responsibility. Most important, we learned that all of us do indeed inhabit *one* planet. We felt wonderful about ourselves.

Notes

[1]Sunbear and Wabun, *The Medicine Wheel* (Englewood Cliffs, New Jersey: Prentice-Hall, 1980).
[2]Robert Hofsinde (Gray-Wolf), *Indian Sign Language* (New York: William Morrow & Company, 1956).
[3]Hyemeyohsts Storm, *Seven Arrows* (New York: Ballantine Books, 1972).

Resources

1. *Eastern Indians.* An annotated bibliography with emphasis on indigenous tribes of Connecticut. Compiled and edited by Connecticut Indian Educational Council, Inc., Indian Advisory Committee, under the auspices of Connecticut State Department of Education.
2. The American Indian Archaeological Institute is an excellent resource. It is an exciting place to visit and their Education Department has books, films, articles, and an extensive bibliography. The address is

   P.O. Box 260
   Washington, CT 06793
   (203) 868-0518
3. Eagle Wing Press, Inc., Naugatuck, Connecticut.

Oh, yes, I went to the white man's schools. I learned to read from school books, newspapers, and the Bible. But in time I found that these were not enough. Civilized people depend too much on man-made printed pages. I turn to the Great Spirit's book which is the whole of his creation. You can read a big part of that book if you study nature. You know, if you take all your books, lay them out under the sun, and let the snow and rain and insects work on them for a while, there will be nothing left. But the Great Spirit has provided you and me with an opportunity for study in nature's university, the forests, the rivers, the mountains, and the animals which include us.

Tatanga Mani, a Stoney Indian

CHAPTER 4

INTEGRATION:

AN INFORMAL APPROACH TO TEACHING PRIMARY SOCIAL STUDIES

Lise Melancon and Suzanne Peters

At Indianola Informal Alternative School, each classroom is a family group containing two grade levels (Suzi—grades K and 1; Lise—grades 1 and 2). Since the school is an alternative school, children from all over the city are chosen by lottery to attend; therefore the children represent a wide variety of ability and socioeconomic backgrounds.

The philosophy of our informal classroom is built primarily on a firm knowledge of child development and learning theories. The program provides a fully integrated curriculum in which there is a free flow between subject areas reflecting the interrelatedness of all human knowledge. The informal learning environment stimulates exploration, manipulation, and firsthand experience. We emphasize problem solving, autonomy, and independent thinking by providing alternatives and real, practical experiences along with adult guidance and social interaction.

We try to guide children from egocentricity into understanding themselves and the feelings and rights of others. The fundamental purpose is to help children work out problems wholly or partly on their own and ultimately to become individuals capable of knowing right from wrong and of making intelligent, reasoned choices. Informal education deals with *real* problems, *real* experiences, and *real* people, building concepts and understandings that teach children *how* to learn more than *what* to learn.

Each year, we design a yearlong, thematic unit to integrate social studies with all the disciplines in the district's course of study. Our kindergarten, 1st, and 2d grade children chose this year's unit as a result of an end-of-the-year picnic. One of our kindergarten students found a hole in the shape of a human leg. Thus, "Archaeological Dig: Can You Dig It?" was born.

The purpose of our study was to understand the growth and development of our local cultural heritage. Handed down by ancestors, culture is accepted behavior for a group of people who live together and share the same ways of life. Because America is the home of many cultures, we thought it vital to expose the children to different elements of a variety of local cultures.

After taking a survey of the nationalities represented in our classes, we decided to study African, Appalachian, Hispanic, and Oriental cultures. We chose to focus on the African and Appalachian cultures because we are an urban school district. The Hispanic and Oriental cultures were selected because of their prominence in the neighboring Ohio State University community. We decided to include the Cherokee Indians because of the proximity to the Appalachian area.

Consistent with our informal philosophy, the children's understandings of cultures were developed through hands-on, experiential learning. We taught our social studies unit through decision making, problem solving, mathematics, language arts, resource people, information books, videotapes, films, slides, field trips, and hands-on activities.

Our archaeological dig was done by the 10 kindergartners, 29 first graders, and 13 second graders in our two classrooms. Parents became actively involved in our yearlong study by sharing their cultural backgrounds, teaching crafts, providing crafts materials (to keep our overhead low), attending and supporting our bazaar, and chaperoning field trips which included our Saturday dig.

After selecting the theme for our unit, the next step was brainstorming for concepts to be introduced, ideas to be developed according to the guidelines of our course of study, and specific projects that could be implemented. Then we tried to arrange these thoughts into a logical progression according to the availability of dates for speakers and field trips.

When all of this had been prearranged, a working web was begun, listing field trips and speakers. A month-by-month outline evolved from the scheduled activities. As the year progressed, the children became actively involved in creating, deciding, and completing some of their interests in the language arts and research parts of the web.

In a joint effort to plan the fine arts section, the children helped us by expressing their interests and desires for work in the arts. The end result of all this combined effort, as well as our addition of the required disciplines (social studies, mathematics, science), was the web in Figure 1.

September and October: Digging into Our Own Cultural Backgrounds

In order to encourage children to become more cognizant of similarities in their family backgrounds, we asked them to create family trees. This made them aware of their countries of origin. Since five-, six-, and seven-year-olds tend to be oblivious to life outside their immediate environments, we created an experiential game in which each child brought from home several "artifacts" to bury in our sand box, showing their interests and family backgrounds. By a lottery system, each child was assigned an "Artifact Appreciation" time. After burying his/her own artifacts, the child took the "special shovel" to the two classmates who had been chosen archaeologists for the day. When the artifacts had been uncovered, the children/archaeologists tried to make some guesses about what was important to the child. One child buried a silk scarf to show her Oriental background; another person brought a family Bible to boast of her pride in her roots; a girl hid a Nigerian cookbook to reveal the nature of foods cooked in her home. After completing the artifact activity, we decided to burrow deeper by introducing our Archaeological Dig Game.

Figure 1
THEMATIC UNIT WEB

RESEARCH
1. observation of soil—(What is in the ground?)
2. bees, spiders (insect parts), silkworms
3. four layers of the earth
4. volcanoes, earthquakes, rock formations
5. erosion and its effects on the environment
6. books, trips, literature, films, movies, slides, speakers, videos
7. bee lab—OSU
8. family trees

SPEAKERS
1. Dave Casdorph (beekeeper)
2. Randy Sanders (Ohio flint and tool types)
3. Doris Wipert (ancestor talk)
4. Shirley Hysell (rock collector and artist)
5. Mike Hansen (geologist on Ohio rocks and minerals)
6. Jack Keaton (Smokey the Bear—conservation of the environment)
7. Sally Lee (American Indian from Cherokee tribe)
8. Buggy Martin (spiders)
9. Archaeologist from the Ohio Historical Society (brought his slides from an actual "dig")
10. Vicki and Ricardo Stoddard (Hispanic culture)
11. Parents shared:
   —knowledge
   —artifacts, fossils, rocks
   —craft-making skills
12. Lou Casperson (slides and talk on Kenya and China)
13. Jessie Crook (slides and talk on extended families in China and economics)
14. Dr. Ed Scahill (President of the Council of Economic Education—talks about money)
15. Dr. Ted McDaniel (OSU professor of Afro-American music—presented a concert)
16. Dr. Gilbert Jarvis (OSU professor—spoke on China)

MATH
1. basic skills
2. using rocks:
   (a) count
   (b) classify and sort
   (c) measure
   (d) graph
   (e) weigh and compare
3. economics (barter-trade-money)
4. surveys
5. abacus
6. tangrams
7. patterns
8. marketing skills
9. cooking (measurement)
10. problem solving

FINE ARTS
1. music of cultures
2. dance of cultures
3. art of cultures
4. drama of cultures
5. kite making
6. fossil making
7. origami
8. desert sand painting
9. weaving
10. basket weaving
11. instruments
12. hand sounds
13. records and tapes
14. appreciation of all fine arts of the other cultures
15. calligraphy
16. totem pole making
17. mask making
18. clay bowls
19. Kachina dolls
20. Pagoda Valentine Box Contest
21. gingerbread wall and house building
22. ceramic tiles
23. bead work

LANGUAGE ARTS
1. literature books
2. visit from author ("Vera B. Williams Day")
3. story writing
4. big books
5. charts
6. trade books
7. resource books (information)
8. dictionary work
9. Indian symbols
10. Chinese characters
11. calligraphy
12. chapter books
13. story retelling
14. flannel board activities
15. storytelling elements
16. sense of story

SCIENCE
1. rocks (composition, formation)
2. soils (good or poor quality)
3. environment (how elements affect)

4. erosion
5. insects: bees, spiders, silkworms
6. fossils
7. classification of animals
8. dinosaurs
9. experiments

1. possible dig
2. Cultural Bazaar (economics—donate to charity proceeds from "parent and family night")
3. residency of Appalachian and African dancers (Artists-in-school)
4. create own culture—bury artifacts

<u>FIELD TRIPS</u>

1. Sharon Woods (soil formation)
2. tour of old Franklinton:
   - see mounds, historic sites, landmarks
   - Why did early settlers choose to live in certain areas and not in others?
3. Greenlawn Cemetery:
   - cremation
   - burial ceremonies for cultures
4. State House—downtown fossil hunt and picnic with parents on the State House lawn
5. Indian Display at the Ohio Historical Society
6. OSU:
   - Townshend Hall steps for fossil rubbings
   - Orton Hall geological display
   - Mershon Auditorium—Chinese art pieces
7. Harlem Ballet—Ohio Theater
8. Olentangy Caverns "family" outing and picnic
9. Center of Science and Industry Museum—dinosaur display
10. Art Museum—Chinese and African Art

<u>SOCIAL STUDIES/ECONOMICS</u>

1. speakers
2. resource books
3. encyclopedias
4. trips
5. films, videos, slides
7. literature books
8. "learning" games
9. "day without rules" purpose for laws
10. class discussions
11. class sharings
12. problem solving
13. decision making
14. peer interaction
15. customs of cultures
16. Hispanic culture
17. American Indian culture
18. "Trail of Tears"
19. Chinese culture
20. Afro-American culture

The spaces on this game were footprints which led to pictures of various people on an archaeological dig. Players traveled around the game board by rolling a die. Each time players landed on a dig picture, they drew a card from the deck. The cards contained pictures (that had been cut apart to make a puzzle) of archaeological treasures which the children had to piece together. The goal was to piece the parts together to make a completed artifact, such as an urn. The children were allowed to trade cards with other players. The more adept barterers took advantage of the less skillful. The children also "wheeled and dealt" when they held a card that would complete another player's puzzle. For example, the kindergartners generally traded one for one; some 1st graders "wheeled and dealt" to get the missing puzzle parts. A few 2d grade "card sharks" found strategies to protect and keep puzzle pieces needed by others as well as to use leverage in getting pieces they needed.

November and December: Rules Affect Life and Death

After much discussion of the ways cultures are alike and different, we observed that most of the children believed dead people were buried in a coffin in the ground. On our field trip to the museum, they learned that not just artifacts could be found buried in the earth, but mummies were too! They were shocked to see the wrapped up remains of an Egyptian mummy. This sparked a whole new area of discussion. Children brought in books about death with photos depicting Indian mounds, war cemeteries, cremation, and mausoleums. Throughout this study, we discovered that the law or customs of different cultures determined the means of burial. Because parents were as ignorant about burials as we were, there was a great deal of positive and inquisitive feedback. We all discovered that in death, just as in life, there are rules to follow. (Bodies must be placed feet first in a mausoleum; however, bodies to be cremated are placed head first.)

Because of this interest in customs surrounding death, we decided to let the children discover the reasons cultures have laws and rules. We used the book *Shiver, Gobble, and Snore*[1] to show the consequences of living in a country with no rules. To make the ideas of the book a reality to the children, we decided to experience a day without rules in our classrooms. They were enthusiastic about the day until their freedoms were infringed upon (for example, a pencil was broken; children were interrupted by another child; their computer time was stolen by a more aggressive child; items brought in for sharing were taken). When the children came to us with complaints, we sat back and calmly said, "Sorry we can't help you. There are no rules in this country today." Their enthusiasm for a day with "no rules, no consequences" soon waned, as they realized the golden classroom rule (respect for others) was no longer enforced.

January and February: Following the Yellow Brick Road to Success

The Oriental, Hispanic, African, and Appalachian cultures we studied grouped for economic reasons: they moved from place to place to find food, water, and salt or to find better weather or protection from the elements. Groups that did not have to move about to get food could use the time for trading.

We created a game entitled Trail of Tears (and Tokens) to apply previously learned information about the Cherokee Indians in a relevant situation. Humor was used throughout the gameboard to entice the children to want to continue the game. For example, one square said, "You think you can get Wampum at a Shell Station. Lose one product." Another said, "You stepped in buffalo chips while farming. Lose one product." Still another stated, "Curses, SOILED again! The red clay soil is pretty to look at, but not very good for growing crops. Lose one product." The children needed to use decision making in the game to solve the problem whether to travel west as ordered by the government or to stay behind in North Carolina. As they traveled around the game board, the children gained or lost products ("candy maize") according to the squares they landed on. The game continued until all had reached whichever Cherokee territory they chose.

The Follow the Yellow Silk Road game was created to reinforce the importance of world trade. Each player started with 20 products to trade on the Silk Road of China. The players faced various risks and opportunities along the path of the game board as they competed to return home from the trade route with the greatest number of desired goods. There were two spaces where the players could exchange their goods and return home, thus forgoing hazards further along the path; or the players could risk failure and continue their trading adventure with the possibility of gaining additional products. Mathematics came into play as the children figured how many products they would get by completing the journey and making a 3-for-1 trade (as opposed to the 2-for-1 and 1-for-1 trades at the opportunity cost spaces). In addition to reinforcing math and reading skills, various factual aspects of Chinese culture and history were incorporated to add interest, information, and humor.

Our primary focus with these cultures was to integrate them with art, dance, drama, and music. We solicited the talents of our "Arts Impact" teachers who scheduled Karimi (African folktales and dance) and Shuffle Creek Dancers (Appalachian Culture) for "Artists in the School" week. The children prepared for their arrival by doing map work (location of their cultures), comparing folktales by using literature, recording and reporting on the collected pertinent research, and observing and identifying different dance styles.

March, April, May: Productivity—Backbone of Bazaar

As we dug deeper, we discovered that the people we were studying learned skills from their ancestors. Today most people learn in a variety of formal and informal learning situations. We invited our "skilled ancestors" (mothers, fathers, aunts, uncles, etc.) to share their knowledge on two crafts days. One of our Hispanic families graciously displayed articles from their background, such as blankets, gourd instruments, clothing, and also showed us how to do sand painting.

For one culminating activity, we planned a cultural bazaar. Our goal was to involve the whole family in this evening. The children were asked to display and sell their crafts (made on crafts days) for as much as they felt they were worth. The parents (with prior secretive instructions from us) set out to elicit and good-naturedly appraise the values defined by the children. The teachers, disguised as fun-loving, carefree browsers, actually were informally assessing the fruits of their labors. We began by analyzing the interaction and communication skills taking place between buyer and seller during this simulation of an African market. As we strolled through the marketplace, we measured the success of our teachings by listening to the rationale used by the children in evaluating the quality of their craftsmanship.

The next day at circle time, we concluded the evaluation of our cultural studies by posing interpretive questions that could be answered by each child at his/her level. (For example, What were the pitfalls of the bazaar? How could we have improved the situation? If you were an archaeologist trying to find out the uses of obsidian, which culture would you be more likely to study about? As an adult, would you like to live and work in one of these countries we learned about? What were the reasons that some crafts didn't sell? Did the location of your market affect how many of your goods were sold? Would you rather be a boy or a girl growing up in one of these cultures? Why? Are they treated equally?) After collecting data by observing, questioning, listening, and then synthesizing, we felt comfortable in concluding that our unit was a success.

Throughout the nine months of our study, we provided situations for the children to apply creative and critical thinking, problem solving, and decision making. We abode by the Chinese proverb, "I hear . . . and I forget. I see . . . and I remember. I do . . . and I understand." For example, to foster children's ability to apply previous knowledge to a new situation, we set up an experiment in which the children had to use problem solving. They were given actual pottery pieces to compare and contrast what they had learned from discussions and books. Bits of pottery buried in a pile of sand became lessons in Indian culture as students figured out what kind of vessel they came from, how the vessel was used, and what it showed about the culture. Math skills came into play as they tried to figure out the circumference of the vessel. They practiced reading as they researched the culture, and practiced writing as they recorded their discoveries.

During our Indian study, the children were given specific commodities which they had to trade with other tribes in order to survive. For example, at lunchtime, one tribe was given all milk while the other tribe was given all food. The "milk tribe" suddenly became very aggressive traders. The "gut level" meaning of interdependence hit a vulnerable spot.

One example of planning in our Cultural Bazaar occurred when the children discussed how to display their calligraphy (made on brown Kraft paper using water color paints for the Oriental characters), which they made on Crafts Day. The procedures we witnessed as more children wanted to help were as follows. At first the children who wished to participate assumed a job. When several children wanted to do the same function, Darin (the planner) decided where the helpers would be. If there was opposition to his plan, Darin fired them! This emergent leader formed an assembly line in which Elise counted out four calligraphy cards, Hilary put them in an envelope, Stevie tied yarn around the envelope, and Angel held a finger on the yarn to help form a bow. Darin was so tenacious in his supervisory role that we thought we had a young Lee Iacocca on our hands!

Our Cultural Bazaar gave us many chances to gain experiences in mathematics. At their open-air "African markets," children had the option of selling their wares to middlemen (teachers) for faux money. We arranged payday so that children had to calculate the amount owed to them. These children didn't need an abacus, a calculator, or even their fingers and toes. As a result, the abstract concept of place value when related to this experience became real for the children. We believe children are not different from adults when monetary incentive is involved.

For our final activity of the year, we made arrangements with the Licking County Archaeological Landmarks Society to go on a real dig. The society was pleased to reward us with this special day, since our children donated two hundred dollars from the proceeds of the Cultural Bazaar!

We gathered at our school early one Saturday in May. We formed a car pool–caravan to travel to the Murphy Prehistoric Site in Granville, Ohio. Parental enthusiasm was as great as children's excitement. Ohio archaeologists had been excavating this site for the past three years and had learned much about the burial practices of these people.

Our teaching methods paralleled the work done by archaeologists. Before we began fieldwork, research was done; during fieldwork, we applied what we knew; after the fieldwork was completed, we analyzed and interpreted what we discovered.

Our informal approach to teaching social studies creates a positive, creative, challenging atmosphere in which the teacher continues to grow along with the children. Self-esteem is nurtured in this low-risk, safe environment, and as we all know self-esteem is the key to success in real life.

Note

[1]Marie Winn, *Shiver, Gobble, and Snore.* (Simon & Schuster, Inc., 1987).

CHAPTER 5

WHERE HAVE ALL THE HEROES GONE?

Jessie B. Crook

S everal years ago, I received a copy of *Junior Scholastic* magazine (December 13, 1980) that included the article "What Makes a Hero?" The author reported that most young people idolize sports figures, entertainers, cartoon characters, or "superheroes." Persons such as Martin Luther King, Jr., or Thomas Edison did not come to mind as persons admired by students. For me, this article became a challenge. How could I help my students become sensitive to the contributions made by people who choose to live their lives for others—people who decide to make a difference in the lives of other people? I had already included work on American Heroes in my 6th grade classes in Columbus, Ohio, using a unit on Famous Americans. I had become increasingly dissatisfied with the unit and had been working to include improved ways for developing thinking skills through independent research. The *Junior Scholastic* article provided the impetus.

I began the unit by asking students to write the names of persons they admired on the chalkboard. I then asked student volunteers to underline the names of all entertainers, circle the names of sports figures, and draw a wavy line under the names of any others. As the *Junior Scholastic* article predicted, most persons listed were entertainers and sports figures. In each of my three classes, however, one or two students listed persons such as Harriet Tubman or Helen Keller. That helped me guide the students to a definition of a hero with such questions as, "Which of these persons made contributions that positively affected the lives of a certain group of people or of people everywhere? Which persons seem to have been motivated to live their lives for others?" Through class discussions which in no way lessened the contributions of sports figures and entertainers, students were guided to a definition of *hero* as a person—man or woman—who has made or is making a positive difference in the lives of others. We discussed the word 'heroine' and agreed that 'hero' would refer to a man or woman in our unit of study.

Differing Ways to View Life Choices

Having students read the *Junior Scholastic* article helped me to begin to achieve a major objective: To help students to an awareness that there can be other good reasons for admiring persons than fame and wealth. This is a delicate value judgment, but I am convinced that students need to know of differing ways of viewing life choices. Too often, the drive for material wealth is the basis for important decisions. I wanted students to develop admiration for diverse life choices and be aware that commitment to goals that help others is worthy of admiration.

As we developed a list of persons who fitted our definition of *hero,* it was clear that it would not be easy to wean some students away from a study of their favorite entertainer. One year, two girls were adamant that they just *had* to study and report on Michael Jackson. Since compromise is a familiar tool in dealing with 6th graders, I proposed a combined study of Michael Jackson and Jesse Jackson. The girls agreed to research and compare the contributions of each. From their research they developed fine posters, maps, and news clippings showing the life of each Jackson. Even though their oral presentation heavily favored Michael, they were able to highlight the leadership qualities of Jesse Jackson and his work to help young people achieve.

Presentations

Just as the list of heroes studied varied, so too did the quality of the presentations. Some students went to great lengths in preparing costumes and props. One student—a zealous Boy Scout—had studied Daniel Carter Beard, who was instrumental in establishing the Boy Scouts in the United States. The student built a paper and wood replica of a campfire. A small group of boys sat around the campfire with marshmallows on sticks while "Daniel Carter Beard" told stories of his life. The boys had been prompted to ask leading questions so "Beard" could tell about himself and his achievements. This was a creative and rather elaborate presentation. Some students were just as successful in presenting their research findings with a single prop—maybe a hat, scarf, or cane. Most important, every student had something to contribute regarding his or her hero on the final presentation day.

Skills Development

Much student success in this unit derives from the fact that a study of one's hero is intrinsically motivating. Yet even the most highly motivated can lose interest as information and materials are gathered, evaluated, and molded into a presentation. Our most difficult trick has been to balance twelve-year-old enthusiasm with teacher demands for "quality" independent work. The unit provides ample opportunity for student growth, in such seemingly mundane skills as note taking, paraphrasing, and map reading, as well as the more abstract skills of analysis, synthesis, and evaluation. How can we infer the personality traits of our heroes from our reading? How can we present a person to the class? What do we mean by 'hero' and how can I justify my hero to the group?

At the risk of dampening student enthusiasm, I have developed several student worksheets to help focus student work and learning as well as ensure a successful experience (see Exhibits 1, 2, 3, 4 at end of chapter). Each is important in keeping students on track and ensuring timely completion of different segments of the unit. For many of my students, this is one of the first encounters with a large independent project. I believe it is important for students to develop the ability to work independently, to manage study time, and to produce a product—in this case an oral presentation. It is also important that they succeed; the worksheets are intended to help ensure success.

Role-Playing

At the end of extensive research and hard work, students are able to make their final presentation with more confidence and enthusiasm. Middle school–aged students are idealistic, receptive to, and impressed by the good that one achieves with one's life. Rarely does a student do anything but a well-organized and confident final presentation. I believe this is also because role-playing is an activity that adolescents welcome. I had used role-plays many times with the students before the "Heroes Unit." They were familiar with the stage fright that was sure to come from performing before other students and a video camera. They were also familiar with the good feeling of having accomplished something they were fearful of doing. There is no better self-concept builder than choosing and then achieving success.

When first introduced to this unit of study, students agreed that overcoming physical handicaps warranted recognition as a hero. A humorous incident occurred in connection with one student's role-play of Beethoven, who overcame deafness and continued to compose music. The student, who had an avid interest in music, had done an excellent job on her research project. She knew Beethoven's life and music thoroughly. On the final presentation day, when the entire school was made aware of our culminating activity (see Exhibit 5), she was greeted and questioned many times during the morning. First, the principal greeted and questioned her in the library. She was unable to answer his questions regarding the Fifth Symphony. Later in the morning, another teacher quizzed her about the dates of some of her compositions. By lunch time, it seemed she had had enough of the Beethoven questions. When she passed by the cafeteria line worker who asked her about one of her accomplishments, "Beethoven" flashed a card on which was printed: "I can't hear you. I'm deaf!"

It was always with great anticipation that the students and I (dressed as one of my heroes) greeted the day for role-plays. The last few years, I videotaped the presentations. With the tension generated by props management, butterfly jitters from students, and the silence in the room for good sound recording, anything could happen. Humor was usually the result of all that tension. An example of this humor was when "Albert Schweitzer's" cotton balls mustache repeatedly drooped; first one side and then the other. The boy role-playing Schweitzer would firmly press it back in place. Finally the mustache dropped off entirely. Calmly it was laid aside and "Dr. Schweitzer" stated, "This heat is dreadful. I was intending to shave soon anyway."

Enhanced student self-concept is one of several "attitudinal" objectives for my hero's unit. The project has also led to increased student cooperation. Students try out their oral reports on one another, they share information and materials as they research their hero. Students will often serve as "support crew"—as a prompter or a planted question to smooth the presentation. Perhaps most important, students gain a deeper understanding of heroes in relation to society. These attitudes, together with student growth in research and organization skills, have made this unit a most satisfying experience.

Exhibit 1
HEROES UNIT INDEPENDENT STUDY PROJECT

Hero: _____ Student Name: _____

These items must be completed by each student:

- Read two biographies of your chosen hero or read newspaper and magazine articles about your chosen hero. Encyclopedia articles and interviews, when possible, will also fulfill the research requirement for this project.
- Pretend you are your hero as you wear a hat (or maybe even an entire outfit) that your hero would wear as you tell the class about "yourself."
- Draw a map of the United States and/or the world with important places in your hero's life labeled.
- Using a scale map, measure the distance from one important place in your hero's life to Columbus, Ohio.
- Make an illustrated folder for all research notes, the bibliography, and any other materials collected for this project.
- Try to locate a picture of your hero to place on our room bulletin board.

Each student must complete at least one of the following:

1. Make a poster showing important events in your hero's life.
2. Write a play or short skit in which important events in your hero's life are told.
3. Write a conversation between two people about your hero.
4. Make a puppet that represents your hero and have it give a speech to the class.
5. Make a collage of newspaper articles about your hero.
6. Make a mobile of objects pertaining to your hero.
7. Write a song about your hero.
8. If your hero is from the past, write about at least one event that was happening in the United States or somewhere else in the world when your hero lived.
9. If your hero is a modern-day person, write about how your hero is similar to a person you know of from the past.

Project due date: _____

Parent signature: _____

Exhibit 2
JOT LIST GUIDE

Read in magazines, encyclopedias, biographies, newspapers, and any other resource books to find information about your hero. The following guidelines may help you prepare your paraphrased oral presentation:

- Important dates in hero's life
- People important to my hero
- Places my hero lived
- Important contributions of my hero
- Reverses in my hero's life
- Advantages my hero had
- Personality traits of my hero
- Physical description of my hero

Exhibit 3

HEROES PROJECT STUDY PLAN

NAME: _____

MON	TUE	WED	THU	FRI	SAT	SUN
Introduction of "Heroes" Independent Study Unit	Discussion of Heroes Unit	Begin chart paper list of chosen heroes	School library research visit (note taking)	Continue chart paper list of chosen heroes	Research in public library?	
Parent signatures due; final names on hero chart; school library visit	Study plan due	Jot list due	Outline due	Illustrated folders made in class		
		"Independent Work Rate Sheet" as homework	Brief oral progress reports in class			
		Heroes presentations in class (folders due)	Heroes presentations in class	Composite list of heroes' qualities and personality traits		

Study plan due date: _____   Parent signature: _____

Exhibit 4
INDEPENDENT WORK RATE SHEET

NAME _____

The independent project I'm working on is:

_____

_____

The parts of the project I've completed are:

_____

_____

The parts I have to complete yet are:

_____

_____

I plan to complete all of this on time; therefore, I must:

_____

_____

Today's date _____

Project due date _____

Parent signature _____

Exhibit 5
WOODWARD PARK SCHOOL DAILY STAFF BULLETIN NOTE

To Staff and Students:

Today is the culmination of the heroes unit for students in Mrs. Crook's social studies classes. As you see students dressed as their heroes in the halls, lunchroom, library, and at work around the school today, please greet them as the person named on their name tag. We will be scheduling visits to other classes for invited heroes next week. If you would like to schedule one or more of these students to visit your class and speak as their hero, please speak to the student about it as you greet her or him today. Also, put a note in Mrs. Crook's mailbox stating the time you would like the hero to visit. Thanks for helping make this an enjoyable day for Room 101 students.

CHAPTER 6

THE MAKING OF A CONSTITUTION:

SELF-GOVERNMENT SEVENTH GRADE STYLE

Betsy Dudley

It usually does not take long for someone working with junior high school students to broach the issue of responsibility. A former student of mine recently reported having kept track of how often I used the term in a single day. Although I have forgotten the exact number, I remember that it was high—almost embarrassingly high. She quoted several all-too-familiar phrases:

Your parents can help, but you have to take responsibility for your homework.

As the oldest students, you have a responsibility to provide good examples to the rest of the school.

Regardless of what the group is doing, you are responsible for your own behavior.

As a 7th grade U.S. history teacher at the Cambridge Friends School, a K–8th grade Quaker school in Cambridge, Massachusetts, I had introduced the issue of responsibility into the curriculum in many ways. What responsibilities did England have to her colonies and vice versa? Who do you think was responsible for the American Revolution? What would your responsibilities have been as a woman in the early 1800s?

For several years, discussing questions such as these and emphasizing student responsibilities in homework, behavior, and other activities appeared sufficient. Nevertheless, I increasingly found that such phrases as 'giving students responsibility' and 'we teachers give you students a lot of responsibility' stuck in my throat. I tried a new phrase, 'taking responsibility', as the more assertive counterpart of "giving" responsibility and realized with a jolt that all along I had expected students to take responsibilities I chose to give them. I was a strong advocate of decision making by students, but I was stopping short of having them decide areas of their responsibility. Upon reflection, of course, it became clear why I chose the areas for them. The students might make the wrong choices! What if, left to their own devices, they chose to be responsible for after-school jobs but not for homework? What if they decided that they didn't care about influencing younger children responsibly? And finally, wasn't I hired to be responsible to parents for their children's behavior and learning during the 7th grade? What if . . . ?

Allowing Students Choices

At the same time, I could not dismiss the compelling logic of allowing students greater choice. If you want children to learn to walk, you must let them walk alone. If you want students to learn writing, you must let them write. If you want to teach responsibility, you should let students experience responsibility and in the process allow them to choose the areas where they will be responsible!

Most of this pondering took place as we were about to undertake the study the U.S. Constitution and the Bill of Rights in our yearlong history course. This had not been one of my favorite subjects as a student. I distinctly recalled yawning my way through constitutional history both in high school and later in college. The delicacy of the negotiations and the foresight of the people involved in creating the Constitution escaped me. I had felt indifferent to and distant from the events, despite my teachers' enthusiasm for the process and the remarkable document that it produced. The fact that the Constitution had been amended only 26 times in its two-hundred-year history served to raise their respect and my ennui to high levels.

Based on my own personal experience, I was determined that I would make everything I taught vital and relevant to my 7th grade students. As I planned to teach the Constitution, my musings about student responsibility gave rise to an idea. After studying the Constitution and the Bill of Rights, why not have students create their own class constitution? Why not have them design from scratch their own rules and system of governance? Tentatively, I tried out the idea on my colleagues. They were all supportive but they added to my list of anxious *what ifs.*

The Cambridge Friends School is unusual in its encouragement of thoughtful innovations, especially since it includes students at all ages in making decisions that will affect them personally. By the time students reach the Upper School (7th and 8th grades), they are accustomed to teachers' saying, "What do you think of studying . . . ?" Therefore, there was interest but no great surprise when I broached to my 7th grade class the subject of creating their own constitution. As the class discussed the possibilities, their excitement grew. They began their own list of "what ifs," which did little to relieve my nervousness:

What if we decided not to have any P.E. classes?

What if we decided to have *only* P.E. classes?

What if everyone favored a rule but the teacher?

I had already decided that, if the project was to succeed, I should have to give up some control. I would have as much to say as any one student—but no more. This compromise intrigued many students, who spent days discussing whether I would really "let them" do something. There was excitement, but some students showed nervousness as well because they recognized that the system that protected them could change. I reassured them that I would step in—in fact, the whole experiment would be jeopardized—if students misused the project and did anything harmful to themselves or others. The first year of this experiment I bravely, if somewhat uneasily, asserted that I knew they were more *responsible* than that! In subsequent years, I could honestly say that, although I was prepared to intervene, it had never become necessary.

Studying the U.S. Constitution

Things began to happen in the class. As we studied the U.S. Constitution and the formation of a new system of government, students' questions and comments revealed new levels of fascination and insight. Whereas in previous years the Articles of Confederation had generated little interest, the reasons the Articles failed were now personally intriguing:

We should be able to do better than *that*.

How'd they expect it to work if no one had power to enforce the rules?

What if *our* constitution fails?

Who's going to enforce *our* rules anyway?

Each year that I taught the subject, a different part of the Constitution became the focus of attention and a hot topic for debate. One year, students wondered how the Quakers, who believe in building consensus rather than deciding by vote of the majority, had reacted to the Constitution, which after all had been drawn up in Philadelphia, a Quaker center. More specifically, students argued whether *we* should vote in class about issues if the decision *to* vote had not been reached by consensus. In addition, there was always some news item that connected current events with what we were studying. For example, when President Reagan was in the hospital for minor surgery and had to be anesthetized, Vice President Bush stepped in and the line of succession outlined in Article Two of the Constitution made sense. "Irangate" led to discussions about the powers of Congress and the system of checks and balances. I was struck again and again by the energy with which twelve-year-old students tackled the same information—and made sense out of it—that had baffled and bored many older students, including me!

By the time students had finished the study of the U.S. Constitution, they were eager to start work on their own document. The first step in the process was simple: each student made a list of rules and responsibilities for inclusion in our constitution. As in Philadelphia, there were some limitations. We could not decide, for instance, that 3d graders could not use playground facilities that we wanted to use or that the mathematics teacher had to give shorter assignments. Suddenly, the idea of "taxation without representation" took on new meaning.

We also discussed the limitations imposed by "higher law." The delegates in 1787 felt ultimately responsible to God and their consciences. We, on the other hand, had a Quaker Board of Trustees, parents, faculty, and the Massachusetts Department of Education as our higher law. After some good-natured, and largely exaggerated, groans at the realization that classes, the Quaker Silent Meeting, and homework could not be banned, students set about creating lengthy lists of what they wanted. There was no secret about what was on those lists. I encouraged students to talk to each other and to other people as well so that they could start thinking about the various "articles" that would be part of this new constitution.

Group Tasks

On the day the individual lists were due, I divided the class into groups of four. Each group had three tasks: (1) to choose a clerk or note taker; (2) to go over each person's list, discuss each item, and come up with a common list; and (3) to select a delegate from their group. Coming up with a common list added a component. Since we were a Quaker school, important decisions throughout the school were made by consensus rather than by vote taking; therefore, everyone in the group had to agree on each article that was on the group's list. This slowed the process considerably, but it forced students to think about both the content of a right or responsibility and how it needed to be carefully worded as well.

The choice of a delegate had the same stipulation—no voting. If more than one student wanted to be a delegate, a way to select one person had to be found by the group. Groups would often decide by consensus to draw names from a hat. One year when two people in a group of four each wanted to be a delegate, the group decided that each of them had to give a speech about why the *other* person would be a good delegate. In the process, the one giving the speech convinced herself that the other would be a better delegate. However, this happened only once.

Although the idea of consensus building has its foundation in Quakerism, the practical results of this process can be advantageous in any school. Students really have to *discuss* points, put forth their ideas, defend them if they feel strongly about them, listen carefully to each other, and compromise. Great care has to be taken to word articles accurately and clearly so that no ambiguities will cause trouble later on and so that the results will be agreeable to everyone. Benjamin Franklin might have enjoyed eavesdropping on these bargaining sessions, although he might also have been perplexed by some of the issues. "I'll tell you what. If you support my chewing gum proposal, I'll support your discussion groups during Reading Period."

Abigail Adams, on the other hand, would have had no trouble understanding John's summary of a discussion we had one year. By chance, it happened that all five of the delegates chosen were boys. The uproar was immediate and intense. The boys claimed victory by the luck of the draw, and the girls threatened to boycott the whole operation because they were not fairly represented. Three or four class periods of important and intense discussions followed that would probably not have succeeded if I had set out to plan them.

Fundamental questions were raised. Do men and women represent different interest groups? In what circumstances can one sex fairly represent viewpoints of the other? What happened at the *real* Constitutional Convention? (I thought they would never ask!) What made the situation for women change from 1787 until now? Are women represented fairly in Congress today? Why did it take so long for women to get the vote?

For homework that week, students read material from women's history books, some of Abigail Adams' letters to husband John Adams, and primary sources about women's lives in the late 1700s. This was not the week's agenda, but I am convinced that students learned much from the digression because it sprang from an issue of immediate concern to them. I had hoped for a tidy resolution to the delegate dilemma (based, obviously, on thoughtful discussion, reason, and compromise), but chance, as is often the case in teaching, had the final word. Two of the male delegates caught the flu. Since their alternates were both girls, the class decided pragmatically to get on with business at the expense of tidy resolutions. The final count was three male and two female delegates. Did George Washington ever face such dilemmas?

Class to Accept Articles

During the next phase of the process, each delegate took his or her group's list and with the rest of the delegates repeated the same procedure that the original group of four had followed. All the articles accepted had to be ratified by the whole class. Delegates rotated the responsibility of presenting items to the class and summarizing the pros and cons for each article. Again, we had to reach consensus on each point, and, as a result, many items were tabled temporarily so that people could think about an issue. We became very respectful of how much the delegates to the Constitutional Convention in 1787 had accomplished in only four months.

By this time in the process, some students had considerable ownership invested in certain articles. My role consisted largely of reminding them to listen to one another, respect one another's opinions, and to think about ways a point could be worded so that it incorporated everyone's views. These constant reminders were frequently frustrating—for me and for the students. One year, I happened on something that helped restore my perspective. I looked back at the original individual lists of rights and responsibilities, at the lists the delegates had worked from, and then at the final, ratified articles. It was exciting—indeed exhilarating—to see how the collective process had weeded out the ridiculous and refined the potentially viable proposals. An individual, for instance, had written with great emphasis, "No homework." The group of four had modified that to "No homework on weekends." By the time this article was ratified by the class, it read:

> Whenever possible, homework will be assigned far enough ahead so that people can do it before the weekend. A committee will talk to other teachers about this.

My spirits rose considerably. Despite the higher-law discussion, one tenacious individual had written, "No Quaker Meeting for Worship." The group of four agreed that "We can draw during Meeting for Worship." After several class periods of discussion, the final article read:

> Every third Meeting for Worship we can draw, but all materials have to be together at the start so it does not disturb people *not* drawing. No squeaky or smelly magic markers.

A bit of a stretch from quill pens, but as one student remarked, "This is *our* Great Compromise."

Unanticipated Learning

Sometimes ideas that changed the curriculum unexpectedly came out of the process. One class, for no apparent reason, disliked the thrice-weekly silent reading period. Several individual lists had "No reading period" written on them. Several of these comments were in capital letters with stars and exclamation points for added emphasis. The delegates tempered this wording to a more subtle, "Reading Period is optional."

During the whole group ratification discussion, I probed a bit to see what was so objectionable about reading a book of your own choice for 45 minutes (my idea of heaven, though I did not say so). It turned out that it was not the reading period as such that students objected to but their perceived lack of time to talk in a group about things that were on their minds.

Their idea of heaven, it turned out, was to have 45 minutes a week where they could compare notes about protective parents, irritating siblings, or disloyal friends with an adult present who could set guidelines for conducting discussion but not necessarily determine the topics for discussion. It sounded reasonable to me, and after ironing out a few details, the final article read:

> One of the three silent reading periods each week will be used for Discussion Groups. The Discussion Groups will be optional, co-ed, and attended by [the teacher], though the choice of topic will be up to students. This means that students in reading period have to be quiet since [the teacher] won't be there.

This particular article was the catalyst for a later discussion about a possible amendment to our constitution. The Discussion Group worked extremely well, but the few students who opted for the reading period seemed unable to handle the lack of supervision. All agreed that they liked the new arrangement except one disgruntled student. In the course of the discussion about behavior during the reading period, we discovered that he had been absent the day this article was ratified. He felt that he had been left out of the decision-making process and was, therefore, justified in ignoring the agreement. We gave him a second chance to agree, and the others a chance to reaffirm the decision. That resolved the problem. I wondered aloud whether the state of Rhode Island, the only state not to attend the Constitutional Convention, had felt equally left out.

During the several years that my 7th grade classes have made up their class constitution, there have been many suggestions about variations and additions. Some of these were incorporated into the process; some were excellent suggestions that, unfortunately, did not fit our school's size. For example, the idea of a larger-scale student government—complete with checks and balances, elections, and (especially) a court system—was always intriguing. The various classes consistently decided that this was a cumbersome system of governance for 24 students, but the discussions that led us to that decision were important ones. They reflected how much students had learned about the structure of our national government, and it started them thinking about the purpose of structure.

Results

It would be misleading to think that, once the rules were ratified, everyone followed them without fail. Every year, students passed a chewing-gum rule. The rest of the school was not allowed to have gum, and after lengthy discussions about the risks of flaunting privilege, the ratified article generally read something like this:

> Seventh graders can chew gum during breaks and lunch in the classroom. We can also chew it during reading period and study hall, but we can't blow bubbles then. Infraction of this rule could cause the privilege to be rescinded.

Students were never able to keep within these boundaries, and legitimate complaints from other students and teachers always collected. Meetings would be called, but since I always turned down the offer to monitor students' gum-chewing, a way had to be found to enforce the rule. One year, "gum monitors" were chosen. Sometimes signs were posted at the classroom's exits. Frequently, someone would call out a warning at the end of a break or lunch. The students as a group realized that they needed to solve this problem. This was a far cry from passively listening to me lecture about the necessity of being responsible.

As this project evolved, it became an effective and relevant tool for teaching junior high students about the U.S. Constitution and about the issue of responsibility. Students came to appreciate what the Founding Fathers must have gone through, and why, for instance, some individual state's issues were compromised in order to unify the whole. They also learned firsthand the positive effects of group process, of how the collective mind of a class can temper, modify, and ultimately strengthen an individual's ideas. They proved, certainly to me, but more importantly to one another and to themselves, that being responsible need not be a burden imposed by the adults in their lives. This was an exciting and empowering step in their process of becoming adults.

CHAPTER 7

THINKING, VIEWING, AND DECIDING:

STRATEGIES IN UNITED STATES HISTORY

Kevin O'Reilly

"The unleashed power of the atom has changed everything save our modes of thinking."—Albert Einstein

"Just the facts, ma'am."—Sgt. Friday, "Dragnet"

"We should nuke Iran."—A student

As social studies teachers, we are charged with sensitizing students to the complexity of issues and equipping them with the skills necessary to make intelligent choices about those issues. It is a tall order, and in many cases it means overcoming years of memorizing facts. The task is complicated further by the effects of television. Children form many judgments about the world from television. Even children who are skeptical of what they read may fail to question what they see on television.

Teachers sometimes add to the difficulties by showing films, filmstrips, and videotapes without questioning interpretations set forth in them. We use them as multimedia textbooks without recognizing that these media may be far more influential than texts. We seldom examine these persuasive techniques or explore the influence of media in our lives.

This article describes a curriculum in United States history designed to teach students critical-thinking, critical-viewing, and decision-making skills, and to create a classroom climate that promotes open-minded inquiry.

Critical Thinking

United States history, like all history, is a rich landscape dotted with interpretive questions. What factors led to the Salem witch trials? How radical was the American Revolution? How did slavery affect the personalities of slaves and their owners? Why did the United States enter World War I? What caused the Great Depression? Was the United States justified in dropping the atomic bomb on Japan in 1945?

We wanted to provide students with a variety of perspectives on these and other interesting historical topics. With few exceptions, however, high school textbooks in United States history provide but one perspective on all topics—that of the author. The exceptions didn't provide the kind of interpretations we were looking for, so we wrote 1- to 5-page summaries of historical interpretations found in scholarly books and articles.[1] On each topic we included two or more conflicting viewpoints by historians, calling them Historian A, B, C, and so forth. Thus, students in our curriculum encountered arguments of several historians: Lois Carr and Lorena Walsh on colonial women; Stephen Nissenbaum and Chadwick Hansen on the Salem witch trials; Bernard Bailyn, Louis Hacker, and Edmund Morgan on the American Revolution; Charles Beard and Forrest McDonald on the Constitution, Stanley Elkins, Robert Fogel, and Kenneth Stampp on slavery; Peter Temin and Milton Friedman on the causes of the Great Depression; Gar Alperovitz and Herbert Feis on dropping the atomic bomb; and others. The students didn't know the historians' names, but they knew the arguments and they learned that reasonable people disagree on historical events.

The reading in Figure 1 is an example of a summary we wrote of a revisionist interpretation of the origins of the cold war based primarily on an article by historian Barton J. Bernstein.[2] Students must evaluate the strength of the argument based on their assessment of the reasoning and evidence presented in the reading. The two notes included are Bernstein's. An analysis of the reading in Figure 1 follows later in this article. In our curriculum, this reading is followed by Historian B, a conflicting traditionalist interpretation summarized primarily from historian Martin Herz's *Beginnings of the Cold War.*

To help students develop skills necessary to analyze interpretations, our program has developed a structured series of problems and worksheets. It also includes a "Guide to Critical Thinking" which contains information on the elements of arguments, models of analysis, and guidelines for specific critical-thinking skills. The guide explains that evidence is what establishes premises, and reasoning is what is used to derive conclusions from those premises. The problems and worksheets introduce and break down the skills and give students practice in employing the skills.[3] Each skill is introduced by a concrete problem to make it easier for students who are concrete—rather than formal—thinkers.[4]

Space does not allow more than cursory explanation of the materials and procedures for teaching a few skills. They have been explained in greater detail elsewhere.[5] This article focuses on four: skills in evaluating evidence, causal arguments, comparisons, and generalizations.

Evaluating evidence may begin with a role-play of a robbery in which testimony is given about identifying the thief and the class questions the role-players. After the formal questioning, the class begins to focus on the skill of evaluating the evidence they have heard. In this stage, we are thinking about how we think, about the process for deciding.[6] Specifically, what criteria can we use to decide the quality of evidence? Why did students believe some items of testimony and not others? Are the reasons logical or psychological? Students have always been able to suggest two or three criteria for evaluating evidence. One list of criteria we made into a poster was the following (Figure 2):

Figure 1

Historian A

The United States, not the Soviet Union, bears primary responsibility for causing the cold war. At the Yalta Conference, Joseph Stalin, the Soviet leader, made it clear that he wanted the Soviet Union to have a sphere of influence in Eastern Europe to protect against any future invasions by Germany. If millions of people had just been killed in the United States because of an invasion, we would have tried to protect our borders, too.

Within their sphere in Eastern Europe, the Soviets allowed considerable freedom in 1945 and 1946. Free elections were held in several countries. Bulgaria's elections under Soviet occupation were declared to be the freest in the country's history.[1] Communist candidates were elected in many areas because of their popularity, especially with the peasants.[2]

The problems started when Harry Truman took over as president in April 1945. He self-righteously attacked the Soviets for their domination of Eastern Europe, but he said nothing about the American sphere of influence in Latin America. Backed by the atomic bomb, he tried to intimidate Stalin. The United States even began to rebuild Germany—the thing the Russians feared most!

The Soviets began to tighten their grip on Eastern Europe in response to American threats, although they still allowed considerable freedom in some of the countries. Then, in 1947, President Truman declared cold war on the Soviet Union. In the Truman Doctrine, he said the Soviets relied on terror and oppression and were threatening the world. The Soviets now clamped down tight on Eastern Europe to protect themselves against the United States' threat. American threats had brought on the cold war.

Notes

[1]"He [Soviet Foreign Minister Molotov] read a press report taken from the *New York Times* concerning the orderly fashion in which the elections in Bulgaria had taken place. He said no one could deny the fact that there was wider participation in these elections than in any other in the history of Bulgaria." U.S. Department of State. *Foreign Relations Papers of the United States,* 1945, vol. 2, 731.

[2]"To most people in war-devastated Eastern Europe, rapid economic reconstruction was the most vital issue, even more so than politics. And to a majority of them, state planning (that is, Communism) appeared necessary and logical." Zbigniew Brzezinski, *The Soviet Bloc,* 1960, 7.

Figure 2

Evaluating Evidence

P – Primary or secondary?
R – Reason to lie or protect oneself?
O – Does other evidence say the same thing as this evidence?

The students then fill in worksheets containing such questions as the following (Figure 3):

Some students have had difficulty with the questions in the above worksheet. They may not have known what makes something a primary source or when someone has a reason to lie. We can turn to a worksheet that breaks this skill down even further (Figure 4).

Notice that in each worksheet familiar examples are paired with historical examples. After several repetitions of such worksheets, students try to evaluate evidence presented in interpretations (identifying the evidence is a separate skill). They are also required to include one or two pieces of evidence in the essays they write and to assess the strength of their evidence.

Causal arguments are introduced by asking students what caused something, such as why someone is ill, why an engine won't start, or why a baseball team didn't do well this year. Their answers are causal arguments. The first answer given is written on the chalkboard. For example, "The engine won't start because the choke is not working." This argument is then questioned: How strong or complete is this explanation of the cause? (It has a measure of plausibility, but other possible explanations may have greater plausibility.) A second example is written on the board: "Whenever I study for math tests, I don't do well, so I'm going to stop studying." Here, there is no reasonable connection between the proposed cause (studying) and the effect (low scores). Further-

Figure 3

Strengths and Weaknesses of Evidence

Give the strengths and weaknesses for each item of evidence below:

1. Rita, Larry, and Nella say Cliff definitely stole the bike because they all saw him take it.

   Strengths   Weaknesses

2. A newspaper article in 1865 reported that, according to a mill owner, the working conditions in the Lowell mills in the 1840s were very good.

   Strengths   Weaknesses

Figure 4

Primary Sources/Reason to Lie

A. A primary source is evidence given by a person present at or part of the event reported on. Or it is an object that was part of the event. Put a 'P' next to each item that is a primary source. Ask whether the person doing the reporting was part of the event or saw the event reported on. If so, it is a primary source.

_____ 1. Terry said she saw Derek buy the sneakers.

_____ 2. In his book, *The American Dream* (1977), Lew Smith said Marquette was a great explorer.

B. People have reason to lie when doing so makes them or their group look good or otherwise promotes their interests. They have no reason to lie if doing so makes them look bad or makes their enemy look good. Put an 'R' next to each item in which the person has a reason to lie.

_____ 1. Bill said he didn't steal the radio.

_____ 2. The Pilgrims said they would not have survived without the help of friendly Indians, such as Squanto.

---

more, other antecedent conditions exist that are more plausible causal candidates.

Examination of these two examples leads to discussion of the evaluation of causal arguments in general. Two important questions emerge: (1) Is there a reasonable connection between the proposed cause and the effect? (2) Are there other possible causes that could have yielded this effect?

Some students need more guidance than this. They may have difficulty differentiating between cause and effect or following all the steps in analyzing the arguments. The visual model (Figure 5) has proved helpful for some students.

We discuss how causal reasoning can be used to probe questions of motive (reasons for actions) as well as causes for events. We deal with other aspects of causation also, such as correlations, necessary vs. sufficient conditions, and predicting effects, where the evaluation question is: Are there other possible outcomes than the one predicted?

Comparisons are introduced by telling the class that Pete had a faster time than they did in an automobile race, so Pete is a better driver. What would they ask? (Was he driving the same kind of car? Was it the same kind of race?) Students seem to know the evaluative question to ask for comparisons: How are the two cases different?

There are several types of *generalizations*. In this curriculum, we are primarily concerned that students learn that what is true of an observed subpopulation may not be true of the population as a whole.

Figure 5

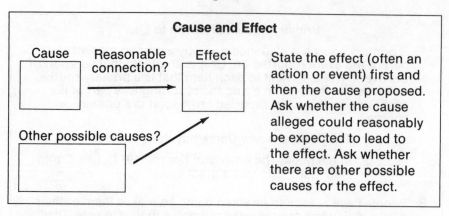

Cause and Effect

Cause Reasonable connection? Effect

Other possible causes?

State the effect (often an action or event) first and then the cause proposed. Ask whether the cause alleged could reasonably be expected to lead to the effect. Ask whether there are other possible causes for the effect.

Generalizations are introduced by asking students what they would infer if they bit into a pizza and found the bite was cold. (The whole pizza is cold.) Evaluative questions have been phrased differently by different classes but essentially they have inquired, How representative is the sample? The concrete example stuck with several students who, whenever they encountered generalizations, exclaimed "Cold pizza!" and then set about to evaluate the generalization.

Using such skills as the four above, students gain some idea of what to look for in interpretations. For the interpretation of the origins of the cold war in Figure 1, students individually and then in small groups should be able to suggest two or more of the following:

1. The evidence in footnote 1 is a quotation by a Soviet leader of a secondary source. Also, the words 'orderly' and 'wider participation' in the footnote were changed to 'free' in the text of the argument.
2. The evidence in footnote 2 is from a secondary source.
3. In the analogy in the third paragraph between Soviet domination of Eastern Europe and American domination of Latin America, is the domination of the same type? Some historians, such as Historian B in this curriculum, argue that Soviet domination—including secret police, one-party control, and widespread human rights violations—was much more severe than American domination.
4. The cause-and-effect reasoning in the fourth paragraph (that since the Soviets tightened up on Eastern Europe in 1947 after the Truman Doctrine) does not provide any evidence to establish the connection between U.S. policy and Soviet control of Eastern Europe. Also, there are other possible reasons for tightening up. For example, maybe the Soviets were experiencing control problems in Eastern Europe.

The above techniques focus student attention on a few broad areas of reasoning rather than a multitude of fallacies. This more general focus seems to work well.[7]

These analytical and evaluative skills are not used just for evaluating interpretations. Students can use the skills for making their own reasoned judgments in classroom discussions and in their writing. We can move to activities in which we give students information and ask them to form their own hypotheses.[8] In other problems, students gather the information and then form hypotheses. All these activities are designed to promote the view that history is a series of hypotheses or theories, not unchallengeable conclusions.

The step-by-step method helps students master certain skills, but it must be combined with other, less prescriptive activities. Without flexibility, we might limit student thinking and degenerate into right-answer methodology. Students should be encouraged to note strengths or weaknesses of arguments that we have not covered as skills. Students are also given essay assignments without reference to particular critical-thinking skills. If students are to be open to new points of view, we have to set an example by being open to different modes of analysis.

To encourage the process of inquiry, one unit on civil rights was set up in which the students wrote an essay and kept a journal—there were no tests. Readings were put on reserve in the library. Each student initially wrote at least two questions about the Civil Rights Movement, chose a reading, skimmed it, and wrote two more questions. We listed the questions on the chalkboard and discussed what makes a good question for research. The students then researched any one of the questions and wrote their essay.

In the meantime, we performed a variety of activities in class, focusing on unstated assumptions and applying and evaluating events and issues in the civil rights unit analogous to those in previous units. The students kept a journal that enabled them to look at the evolution of their thinking. Students were to make an entry for each class and each reading, summarizing what they learned and recording their reactions. Some students made comparisons to novels they had read in English class or to discussions they had had in other subjects. Many journals contained entries in which the students stated they had changed their minds or altered their opinions about particular topics.

Critical Viewing

One of the activities of the civil rights unit was to view an excerpt from the civil rights documentary series "Eyes on the Prize" about the murder of Emmett Till in 1955. Till, a black teenager, was brutally murdered by two white southerners for saying "Bye, Baby" to a white woman. I asked the class what we could conclude about white southern attitudes in the South in the 1950s from this event. I had barely finished the sentence when a student roared, "Cold pizza!" The class then discussed the danger of generalizing about a whole group of people from one graphic example about only two people of that group. We also discussed what kind of evidence would be needed for better substantiating a claim about southern whites' attitudes in the 1950s. Several students pursued this question in their journals, reporting later to the class on statistical and other evidence they found.

The "cold pizza" comment indicated that at least a few students had transferred a critical-thinking skill to a new area—audiovisual media (hereinafter called media). All the critical-thinking skills, including evaluation of evidence, causal arguments, and comparisons—apply to media interpretations. But there are other factors involved in media that need to be analyzed as well.

The authors of media presentations make their arguments in three ways—using logic, sound, and picture. In a videotape on the Vietnam War,[9] the argument is made that Ho Chi Minh as the father of his country's independence movement is analogous to George Washington and American independence. While this claim is being made, a slide of Ho Chi Minh is shown, followed by a slide of George Washington, and fife music is played. A person could reject the analogy based on its logic, but subconsciously continue to associate Ho Chi Minh with George Washington because of the pictures and the fife music. The class discusses these types of subconscious associations in an attempt to subject them to rational analysis.

We also examine individual pictures from the Vietnam videotape for their emotional impact. Students are asked to record what emotions they feel after looking at individual slides. Subsequently, they are given a particular point of view and assigned to write a narration for that slide. We were all amazed that the same airplane looked like a civilian plane with one narration and a military plane with a different narration.

Asking students how viewing is different from reading focuses on how the medium shapes the message. Can they go back and analyze the arguments? How do commercial breaks affect viewing? How does the need to be entertaining shape what is covered, shown, and reported?[10]

Near the end of the Modern United States History course, we discussed various techniques used in political advertisements. On the final examination, the students watched a one-minute political advertisement for John Glenn and wrote an analysis of it. They noticed several techniques that I had failed to notice. These critical-viewing skills are essential in a democracy where 80 percent of congressional and senate campaign money is spent on campaign commercials and where 45 to 65 percent of the people get virtually all their news from television.

Decision Making

Of course, we want students to use critical-thinking and critical-viewing skills to become better decision makers. History provides an unlimited number of decision-making problems. After reading *Thinking in Time*,[11] I felt that decision making was much more complicated than the simple decision-making model we had been using. Of primary importance is the need to identify many types of decision making: personal (deciding whether to get married), international crisis (Cuban missile crisis), bureaucratic (you have just become social studies chair at a new school), economic (Dodge Aries or Mercedes Benz?), and so forth. These decision categories are too different from each other to make a single model helpful.

So students were given several problems and asked to make a decision for each. We then discussed them and listed considerations that might be helpful in making decisions, rather than trying to devise a single, all-inclusive model.

The list was put on a poster in the classroom as a reference for future decision-making problems. Some of the more than 20 considerations were:

- Know the history of the issue.
- Know the background of the people involved.
- Question analogies.
- Get people who have different views of the problem to discuss the problem.
- Set down your goals in the beginning.
- Imagine how this situation will look 25 years from now.

Students might use only two or three of the considerations in any one decision-making problem.

The longest decision-making problem we used was a 10-round computer simulation on the Vietnam War.[12] The students, in groups of three, were given the role of Lyndon Johnson in January 1964 with five decisions to make. Depending on their choices, the computer gave them a new situation for June 1964 and a set of new decisions to make. The simulation continued this way up to June 1968. The purposes of the simulation are to (1) put students through protracted decision making wherein their choices from one round affect later choices, (2) build empathy for real decision makers, and (3) have students discover the relationship of various factors to foreign policy decision making, such as military power, domestic politics, public opinion, intelligence reports, world opinion, big power/client state relationships, and bureaucracies.

Through direct observation, I could see that many students were using the decision-making considerations we had discussed previously. For example, one student said, "But this goes against our original goal of not getting into a 'major' war with Russia or China." Another student mentioned that she asked two students to be in a group with her because she knew they would disagree with her. She wanted to get a variety of perspectives before making her decision.

The students also kept journals for this simulation. The following are excerpts from their journals (the round in parenthesis is the point at which the comment was written):

- "Is it worth losing freedom in the name of peace?" (Round 3)
- "Do all the people in South Vietnam want Communism?" (Round 2)
- "I think we did not discuss our goals enough as a group before we began the simulation." (End of simulation)
- "I wish we could go back in the simulation to change some of our decisions. If we knew the South Vietnamese army was going to be defeated, we would have sent troops in earlier. However, in a way it is good that you can't go back in the simulation. In real life, you can't go back to change your decisions either." (Round 4)
- "I think no matter what decisions we made we were going to be criticized at home. It was a difficult simulation." (End of simulation)
- "I think your priorities must get screwed up when you get powerful—elections and funds start to mean more than people." (End of simulation)
- "I don't think [Vietnam] is any of our business in the first place. But my advisers feel the threat of Communism is too strong." (Round 1)

- "I couldn't believe all the considerations in this decision making; it made it so hard to decide what to do." (End of simulation)

Many students did indeed begin to feel a sense of humility about decision making and an empathy for decision makers. This new attitude should make them more hesitant to gravitate toward simple solutions or make sweeping judgments about decision makers.

Conclusion

The curriculum described in this article is entitled *Critical Thinking in American History*. It is designed to improve student thinking, viewing, and decision making through conscious step-by-step instruction and a more general atmosphere of issue orientation and conflicting points of view. The emphasis is on the process of thinking using the content of history. The aim is to improve student skills and change student attitudes.

Such a curriculum will inevitably invite criticism; it is particularly important to resolve two issues. One must consider the trade-off between content and process. If we spend so much time on thinking skills, the argument goes, students cannot learn very much history. Any teacher can cover more content by lecturing every day. The important question is: What are students actually learning and what will they remember? Since students are confronted with problems to be solved in this program, they are actively seeking information and indeed cover a great deal of content. We believe that, although they may cover less than in a more traditional course, they will retain the information better. Even if we assume that students in this curriculum retain less information, we could ask, So what? Content is important, but so are skills necessary for dealing with content. Students clearly need both.

The second criticism is that students in high school are not developmentally prepared for the formal thinking involved in this curriculum. I have done some evaluation of our program which has shown improvement in students' thinking skills and a more skeptical attitude.[13] However, these evaluations are not conclusive since they were done on small populations and were subject to uncontrolled variables (such as differences in teaching style).

Direct classroom observations[14] indicate that students at all ability levels can learn some of the skills and change their attitudes. In one class of "slow learners," we had a great analytical discussion of the evidence presented in the Bernard Goetz case. At one point a student remarked, "Wait a minute. Goetz must have been facing the other end of the subway car, so how could that witness have seen him smiling?"

In my view, average learners make the greatest progress in learning thinking skills, since honors students already have learned some of the skills by the time they are sophomores or juniors in high school. Average learners also seem to change their view of the nature of knowledge the most. One student asked, "Do you mean everything in this textbook isn't the truth? I don't get it. They paid this guy a lot of money to write this book." That question made the whole year worthwhile. Written feedback from students indicates that a majority enjoy learning the skills and use them in other areas of their lives, especially in writing essays in English class.

Unexpected comments from students indicate they have changed their views and internalized some of the skills. In one class, near the end of the school year, a student brought in and read an article about a local issue. We discussed the article for a minute and then a student said, "Well, that's an interesting article, but I'll bet there is a Historian B out there somewhere with a different opinion."

Notes

[1]Kevin O'Reilly, *Critical Thinking in American History,* 4 vols. (South Hamilton, Mass.: Critical Thinking Press, 1983–86).

[2]O'Reilly, vol. 4, 80–86. The reading has been shortened considerably for this article. Historian A is from Barton J. Bernstein, "American Foreign Policy and the Origins of the Cold War," in *Politics and Policies of the Truman Administration,* ed. Barton J. Bernstein (Chicago: Quadrangle, 1970). Historian B is from Martin Herz, *Beginnings of the Cold War* (New York: McGraw-Hill, 1966).

[3]Barry Beyer, "Teaching Critical Thinking: A Direct Approach," *Social Education* 49 (April 1985): 297–303.

[4]According to Piaget, concrete thinkers are somewhat restricted to what they encounter in direct experience. Concrete thinkers may have difficulty dealing with abstract reasoning such as causal arguments and what makes a strong generalization. The cognitive level of students in history courses has been the subject of debate. Roy Hallam argues that almost all high school students before the senior year are concrete thinkers. Christian Laville and Linda Rosenzweig believe many more high school students are formal thinkers and question Hallam's evaluation. See Roy Hallam, "Piaget and Thinking in History," in *New Movements in the Study and Teaching of History,* ed. Martin Ballard (Bloomington: Indiana University Press, 1974), 162–78; Christian Laville and Linda Rosenzweig, "Teaching and Learning History: Developmental Dimensions," in *Developmental Perspectives on the Social Studies,* NCSS Bulletin 66, ed. Linda Rosenzweig (Washington, 1982): 54–66.

[5]See, for example, Kevin O'Reilly, "Teaching Critical Thinking in High School U.S. History," *Social Education* 49 (April 1985), 281–84.

[6]Arthur L. Costa, "Teaching For, Of, and About Thinking," in *Developing Minds: A Resource Book for Teaching Thinking,* ed. Arthur L. Costa (Alexandria, Virginia: Association for Supervision and Curriculum Development, 1985), 21–23.

[7]The strategy of focusing on a few broad areas is from Perry Weddle, *Argument: A Guide to Critical Thinking* (New York: McGraw-Hill, 1978). He has separate chapters on generality, comparison, and causation.

[8]See, for example, the problem on the Sacco and Vanzetti case in O'Reilly, *Critical Thinking,* vol. 4, 56–58.

[9]This videotape contains two opposing viewpoints of the Vietnam War. They cover the same material and use some of the same slides but present radically different perspectives. The worksheets focus on the media techniques used in the presentations, as well as on the content. Kevin O'Reilly, *Vietnam: A Case Study for Critical Thinking* (Pleasantville, New York: Educational Audiovisual, 1987).

[10]These questions along with a number of other critical-viewing activities are from Kevin O'Reilly and John Splaine, *Critical Viewing: Stimulant to Critical Thinking* (South Hamilton, Mass.: Critical Thinking Press, 1987).

[11]Richard E. Neustadt and Ernest R. May, *Thinking in Time: The Uses of History for Decision-Makers* (New York: Free Press, 1986).

[12]Kevin O'Reilly, "Decision-Making in the Vietnam War," (South Hamilton, Mass.: Critical Thinking Press, 1987).

[13]See O'Reilly, *Critical Thinking,* vol. 1, Teachers Guide, 15–16, for an explanation of the evaluations I have done.

[14]Arthur Costa agrees that in some respects classroom observation is a method of evaluation superior to the quantified results of paper-and-pencil testing. Arthur Costa, "Thinking: How Do We Know Students Are Getting Better at It?" Paper presented at Teaching for Thinking Conference, May 19–21, 1986, Hartford, Connecticut.

References

Bernstein, Barton J. *Politics and Policies of the Truman Administration.* Chicago: Quadrangle, 1970.

Beyer, Barry. "Teaching Critical Thinking: A Direct Approach." *Social Education* 49 (April 1985): 297–303.

Bloch, Marc. "Historical Causation." In *The Historian's Craft.* New York: Random House, 1953.

Costa, Arthur. "Teaching For, Of, and About Thinking." In *Developing Minds,* Alexandria, Virginia: Association for Supervision and Curriculum Development, 1985.

Hallam, Roy. "Piaget and Thinking in History." In *New Movements in the Study and Teaching of History,* edited by Martin Ballard. Bloomington: Indiana University Press, 1974.

Herz, Martin. *Beginnings of the Cold War.* New York: McGraw-Hill, 1966.

Laville, Christian, and Linda Rosenzweig. "Teaching and Learning History: Developmental Dimensions." In *Developmental Perspectives on the Social Studies,* NCSS Bulletin Number 66, edited by Linda W. Rosenzweig. Washington: NCSS, 1982.

Lockwood, Alan, and David Harris. *Reasoning with Democratic Values: Ethical Problems in United States History,* 2 vols. New York: Teachers College Press, 1985.

Neustadt, Richard E., and Ernest R. May. *Thinking in Time: The Use of History for Decision-Makers.* New York: Free Press, 1986.

Norris, Stephen P. "The Reliability of Observation Statements." *Rational Thinking Reports,* Number 4. Urbana: University of Illinois, 1979.

O'Reilly, Kevin. *Critical Thinking in American History,* 4 vols. South Hamilton, Massachusetts: Critical Thinking Press, 1983–86.

O'Reilly, Kevin, and John Splaine. *Critical Viewing: Stimulant to Critical Thinking.* South Hamilton, Massachusetts: Critical Thinking Press, 1987.

O'Reilly, Kevin. "Decision-Making in the Vietnam War." Computer Simulation. South Hamilton, Massachusetts: Critical Thinking Press, 1987.

O'Reilly, Kevin. "Teaching Critical Thinking in High School U.S. History." *Social Education* 49 (April 1985): 281–84.

O'Reilly, Kevin. *Vietnam: A Case Study for Critical Thinking* (videotape). Pleasantville, New York: Educational Audiovisual, 1987.

Paul, Richard. "Critical Thinking: Fundamental to Education for a Free Society." *Educational Leadership* 42 (September 1984): 4–14.

Weddle, Perry. *Argument: A Guide to Critical Thinking,* New York: McGraw-Hill, 1978.

CHAPTER 8

TEACHING ABOUT THE VIETNAM WAR

Michael Huff and Stuart B. Palonsky

General Approaches to Teaching the Social Studies

New teachers often start their careers with a daunting sense of inadequacy. They may feel insufficiently grounded in content, methods of instruction, student discipline, or all three. Mike Huff remembers experiencing some of this apprehension. A master's degree in political science had added subject-matter depth to his undergraduate social studies program, and service in the military had confirmed his suspicions that there was more to discipline than controlling behavior. But neither the army nor graduate school had taught him how to teach social studies.

Mike knew that the models of teaching provided by his university professors had limited applicability in the classroom. He recalls that one of his undergraduate political science professors announced on the first day of class that there would be no discussion in the classroom because students did not know anything. Students were there to take notes and listen; they were not to interrupt the professor any more than they would interrupt a recital at Carnegie Hall.

Indeed, it was true that the students in the professor's class knew little content, but could content be poured into students' minds like water into a pitcher? Mike knew that he was not going into teaching to become a modern version of Dickens' Thomas Gradgrind—to fill students minds up with dates, names, and battle statistics. Social studies teaching had to be more than transmission of facts from the teacher's notes to the students' notebooks. History and social science should be taught in ways that allow students to hold information and ideas up, examine them, and judge their worth and meaning. The goal in social studies is to produce informed, thoughtful citizens. That implies that students should do more than sit quietly and take notes. Students should be encouraged to read, think, argue, and write about a wide range of historic events and social science issues.

Developing Teaching Strategies and Materials

Knowing what he wanted to achieve made it easier for Mike to find out what he thought were appropriate teaching methods. The combination of a good cooperating teacher, and later, a few thoughtful colleagues and a department chair who encouraged experimentation and tolerated failure helped Mike develop a good repertoire of teaching strategies. He says that he has now learned to be eclectic in his teaching and uses anything that works to get students actively involved in considering social studies content.

I try to vary my teaching methods to keep students (and myself) from getting bored. I write out my lesson plans each day. Typically, they include a list of objectives, some general questions I want students to think about, and the reading and writing assignments for the next day. I use an occasional simulation game and research papers. During the course of a typical week, my classes will include some lecture, some discussion days, some writing, some library work, and some debate.

I love debate activities—social studies are filled with controversial topics that lend themselves to conflicting interpretations—but formal debates tend to be overused (in schools) and, as a result, students too often regard them disdainfully. I prefer point-counterpoint discussions, mock press conferences, and other activities that get students to look at controversial issues from conflicting points of view.

On occasion, formal debates, developed like term papers, can be an effective end-of-unit activity. My classes will spend several days in the library gathering data and readying their arguments. Each side prepares a comprehensive statement, engages in cross-examination, and issues a summary. A side typically consists of four students. One makes the opening statement, two cross-examine, and one gives the closing remarks. I limit the number of cross-examination questions and select student listeners who ask questions of each side. Students not involved in the debates serve as judges. They are asked to make written and oral comments. I make sure that every student takes part in at least one debate activity every two marking periods.

Like most teachers, Mike finds himself buried under an avalanche of papers to be read and tests to grade. Nevertheless, he argues that writing is a way of thinking. He encourages students to write rough drafts first and then revise them. Sometimes he comments on the drafts; at other times, students engage in peer reviews of one another's writing. Only the final draft is graded.

The trick is to balance the volume of student writing with my ability to keep up with it. It's a sure bet student work that is poorly critiqued will result in diminished effort on subsequent assignments.

Two techniques that allow me to manage the volume of student writing are the daily summary and assignment rotation. Each day I ask three students to prepare a short summary of the day's lesson. They are asked to write what they learned and what they considered important. On the following day, they read their summaries to the class and we discuss the summaries briefly. By limiting the students to short 3- or 4-sentence paragraphs, I have them focus on the main ideas of the lesson and I try to get them to practice writing clearly, concisely, and often. Everyone gets several opportunities during the (ten-week) marking period to write summaries. For longer essays, I use a rotating assignment system. Not all the students are required to do every essay assignment, but every student completes an equal number during the course of a marking period.

Teaching about the Vietnam War

Like many teachers of his generation, Mike finds teaching about the Vietnam War personally difficult. The events that are still so powerful and influential in his own life took place too long ago to be remembered by his students.

Treatment of those events in most social studies textbooks is not adequate to convey the intensity and conflict of the period.

Mike typically teaches two or three classes of American History II, a year-long course that focuses on 20th-century American history. As part of this course, he teaches a unit on Vietnam that he estimates he has taught at least 45 times. It was easier to teach about Vietnam when it was a contemporary event, when data generated by the public clashes of rhetoric could be examined in class. Presidents and some members of Congress could be counted on as regular sources of support for the war. Antiwar sentiment was easy to find in the speeches of other public figures and in the lyrics of popular music, for example, Buffalo Springfield's "For What It's Worth" and Crosby, Stills, Nash, and Young's "Ohio."

Mike notes that over time his students have grown less and less informed about the events of the war, the reasons for American involvement, and the effects of the war on foreign policy. His students know little about Ho Chi Minh, Dien Bien Phu, Ngo Dinh Diem, Henry Kissinger, or the Gulf of Tonkin. They tend to think about the war in terms of *Rambo* or *Platoon*. Attitudes seemed to have changed, too: "When students in the 1980s told me that the reason the United States did not win the war in Vietnam was our 'failure to use enough firepower,' I realized that we had come a long way from Woodstock."

The unit on Vietnam is designed to get students to analyze U.S. involvement in Southeast Asia and to examine the effect of the war on people and policy. "I have always tried to prepare a balanced unit," Mike says, "exercising care that my own 1960s baggage didn't get into the lesson."

> I try to be patient when students argue that the United States could have inflicted a greater toll on the North Vietnamese population with increased bombing; I try to be logical when they ask why we had to go all the way to Southeast Asia to stop communism when Cuba is so close to home.

Part of the Cold War

The Vietnam War is part of a larger unit on the cold war. Mike's objectives for the Vietnam unit are lofty. He want students to be able to understand the major political, military, and diplomatic events of the period, and he wants them to consider the moral significance of the war. He wants students to be able to explain why the United States got involved in Vietnam and to analyze how the war was conducted. The students should know about the origins of the cold war, the significance of such events as Gulf of Tonkin Resolution and the 1968 Tet Offensive. They should think about the conflict between hawks and doves and examine such ideas as "Vietnamization" and "peace with honor."

Students need to study the geography of Southeast Asia, the economics of Vietnam, and the politics of war, but they should not get lost in the details. Having students "learn the facts" makes it easier for them to understand the concepts and wrestle with the conflicting ideas of the period. Students should keep notes that reflect the complexity of the era and the issues. They need a chronology of events, a glossary of important terms (e.g., 'Geneva Convention', 'Hanoi Hilton', 'ugly American'); and a list of resolved and unresolved questions surrounding the war. For example: Was Vietnam a "different" war? Should we have "nuked" them back to the Stone Age? Was this war immoral? Which wars were moral? Why do people respond as they do to the Vietnam Memorial in Washington, D.C.?

Using Primary Sources

Mike says that for his students, high school seniors, the best place to begin the three-week unit is with consideration of some primary source material about the cold war. "We first read and discuss a few key documents. I have them read Churchill's Iron Curtain speech, Kennan's containment policy, Dulles's view of the 'unholy alliance between Moscow and Peking,' and the Eisenhower speech in which he proposed the domino theory."[1]

Mike teaches in a school that groups students by ability. He admits that the reading level of the material may be too difficult for some of his students.

> For the honors students, I can assign Kennan's 1947 containment article;[2] they don't need help with it. For most students, it is necessary to read it in class. With slower students, we read it paragraph by paragraph, skipping the less essential prose. It takes us about a day and a half to discuss Kennan's article. The concept of containment isn't difficult for them; only the language is confusing. The students find Dulles hard to read. He raises important and inescapable moral issues, but his vocabulary was not chosen with high school students in mind. However, his views of a bipolar world and brinkmanship give students a good sense of American foreign policy under Eisenhower, and then, when they read about the domino theory, the pattern of our increasing involvement in Vietnam starts to make some sense.

> After a couple of days of some pretty tough reading, the students are ready for a break, so instead of reading Kennedy's inaugural address, we listen to a recording and they take notes. I think it is important for the students to hear how he delivers the speech, his accent, his rhetoric. We also look at specific phrasing, some of which is familiar to them and some that they have not heard before. In the daily summary of the class, I ask them to write a synopsis of the speech and indicate the parts that had the most meaning for them.

Mike introduces his students to the political background of the war and discusses Vietnam with them from various Asian perspectives. The class does some map work, looks at the relative positions of the nations of Southeast Asia, China, Japan, and other aligned and nonaligned nations in the area. Mike then switches to the domestic politics of the war.

> I like to set the stage for some debates: Congress versus the president, hawks versus doves, students versus adults. To maintain freshness, I shift characters from year to year. Typically, we include George Ball, J. William Fulbright, Wayne S. Morse, George Kennan, President Johnson, Barry Goldwater, and General Curtis LeMay. Sometimes the debates are framed as a Senate hearing on a specific aspect of the war. Witnesses can include napalm victims; a Vietnamese citizen who would suffer if there were a U.S. withdrawal; a representative of Dow Chemical, the company that manufactured napalm; or a spokesperson for the poor in the United States who argues that the war has diverted attention from domestic problems.

Identifying Sides of the Controversy

Mike tries to have students identify the various sides of the controversy, assemble the arguments used by a particular side, and then make thoughtful judgments. "We are better able to examine the rightness of the arguments after they have been researched by the students in the library and played out in class."

"To vary the assignments, we may stage mock press conferences in which some students are assigned roles as key players in the Vietnam controversy." Other students are assigned roles as friendly or hostile media correspondents. All students spend a day in the library researching the characters who will give the press conference. (Because schools are more manipulable than real life, a press conference could be scheduled to include Ho Chi Minh, Abbie Hoffman, and Henry Kissinger.)

The student "reporters" prepare two questions for each participant, and we conduct a mock conference in class. It takes one full period. As an assignment, the reporters write an article or an editorial based on the information that was presented during the press conference. Students who do not assume a role must write an account of the activity. "At this point in the unit, I expect students to be able to explain the course of events leading to U.S. intervention in Vietnam, and to be able to state arguments for our involvement and for our disengagement. Then we're ready to fight the war."

Mike fights the war by way of videotape. Commercially available tapes such as CBS's *Chronicle of War,* or the PBS Vietnam series, convey the intensity of the combat, the youthfulness of the combatants, and the power with which the war was brought into American homes.

> I run some footage, stop the tape, ask a question or open the class up for discussion, and move on. I want the students to take notes on the content, consider the fairness of the reporting, and notice how the commentary changed over time. We discuss and write about the role of the press during the war and we keep a glossary of terms to help us understand the videos. Typically, students are split between those who think the reporting was fair, reflecting events without bias, and those who think the media performed a disservice to the country through a slanted representation of the fighting. I also remind students that the tapes they are viewing were those broadcast nightly into American homes. It helps them to understand domestic reaction to the war. We discuss whether or not this was appropriate. My students rarely agree; many of the policy conflicts surrounding the Vietnam War are easy to recreate in class.

Group Problem Solving

After viewing footage of the 1968 Tet Offensive, Mike's class engages in some group problem solving. The class is divided into groups of four. They are told to list the options open to the United States after Tet and to select the best option and the reasons for their choice. After each group completes a rough draft of their policy statement, they are asked to read an article by Clark Clifford, Secretary of Defense in 1968. Students revise their positions based on their degree of sympathy for the administration's new position.

Table
TYPICAL DISTRIBUTION OF TEACHING ACTIVITIES FOR VIETNAM
UNIT (17 days total)

Activity	Number of Days
1. Lecture/class discussion	3
2. Videotape/class discussion	3
3. Library Work	3
4. Press conference simulation	1
5. In-class reading of documents/ primary sources/maps	2
6. Group work/writing	2
7. Test and review of test	2
8. Senate hearing simulation	1

As a culminating activity, Mike assigns an essay question to the students. He gives them a quotation: "Vietnam was a noble cause. . . . We failed because we would not allow our forces to win." The quotation is excerpted from two speeches delivered by President Reagan, but Mike does not identify the source. In their writing, students are asked to examine how and why the United States became involved in Vietnam. They are also asked to evaluate the appropriateness of U.S. foreign policy objectives and the extent to which these objectives were achieved.

The Vietnam unit has complex objectives. Students are given a full-period exam on content that includes short-answer and essay questions. Another period is spent reviewing the outcomes of the exam. Press conference reports, group projects, news stories, editorials, and the final essay all become part of the evaluation process. "I want them to master some of the basic facts and concepts of the Vietnam War," Mike says.

> I also hope that I can convey some of the confusion and conflict of the period. I try to steer them away from simple answers. At first, they ask "Was the war good or bad? Were we right or wrong?" It's hard, but I try to lead them to a thoughtful examination of these questions.

> Last year many of my students went to see the film *Platoon* after they had finished the unit on Vietnam. They critiqued it with intelligence and surprising insight. They compared the film with what they had seen and read in class. They recognized the limitations of the film and the difficulty any filmmaker would have trying to represent the war fairly in less than two hours. Not bad, I thought, for a high school class, and I allowed myself to enjoy the private satisfaction of being a teacher.

Notes

[1]For the textbook in this course, Mike uses Thomas A. Bailey, *The American Pageant: A History of the Republic*, 6th ed. (Lexington, Massachusetts: D. C. Heath, 1978). The readings

come from a supplementary text, Thomas G. Paterson, ed., *Major Problems of American Foreign Policy Since 1914*, vol. 2 (Lexington, Massachusetts: D. C. Heath, 1984).

[2]The article originally appeared in *Foreign Affairs* magazine. Entitled "The Sources of Soviet Conduct," it was anonymously written by Kennan under the name of "Mr. X." Kennan argued that, for Stalin, political action was a "fluid stream which moves constantly wherever it is permitted to move." Kennan recommended a "long-term, patient but firm and vigilant containment" policy as the best solution to Soviet expansion.

CHAPTER 9

OPENING MOUTHS AND OPENING MINDS:
THE AMERICAN EXPERIENCE PROGRAM

John Rossi

I enter my 20th year of teaching high school history and the social studies with thoughts that it may be my last. With some hesitation, I am applying to various graduate schools in the hope that a Ph.D. will enable me to train future teachers. I hesitate to abandon the stimulation of creating new curriculum with a team of good friends and the pride in watching students become excited about lessons we have created. The fear of change lurks around the edges of my life. I reflect on the beginning of my teaching career at El Cerrito High School in the San Francisco Bay Area.

I came back to El Cerrito in February 1968 (I had graduated from there five years earlier) under the influence of Edwin Fenton and inquiry social studies. I wanted students to do more than just recite historical facts and memorize famous names and dates. I wanted them to be able to use those facts to understand concepts, to develop critical-thinking skills, and to clarify values. And above all, I did not want to bore students. My task was to motivate, to bring life to students asleep in the corners, to wake up minds to send them out more intelligent than when they walked in. Those are still my goals. I fear that the volumes of recent reports that decry the failure of schools to teach young people history and literature and claim we are losing our cultural memory will produce political pressures to create courses in which only historical knowledge is required, which is not to say that I devalue historical knowledge. Students need to know the historical story first. But good teaching begins—it does not end—there.

Redesigning the U.S. History Program

Shortly after I arrived at El Cerrito, two members of the social science department—Jim McClelland and Robert Burris—invited me to join them in a summer writing project to redesign the U.S. history program. From the summer meeting was born the American Experience course—a conceptual, activity-based approach to American studies that integrated history, government, and economics into a three-semester package. Also from the project was born a commitment to team planning. Ever since that first summer, as new teachers joined the department, the three of us invited them to participate with us as part of the team. What soon emerged was a team of six or seven teachers who began to meet regularly after school, have lunch together daily, and attend local professional meetings. We became a family.

During our initial summer curriculum planning session, our first major decision was to combine history, government, and economics into a three-semester course. This allowed us to choose concepts that cut across disciplines and to develop relationships among the subjects. The three-semester bloc would also allow seniors to take a social science elective in the fourth semester, a pattern endorsed by the 1968 California State Framework.[1] It spawned a series of elective courses including California History, Economics, International Relations, World Cultures, Comparative Governments, Psychology, Anthropology, and Asian-American Studies.

Course Organization

Our second decision was to organize the course conceptually but to sequence the concepts chronologically. We did not want to teach historical trivia; we wanted history to have meaning in the sense that it would examine enduring issues—questions of freedom and authority, unity and diversity, stability and change. We sought to ensure this goal by beginning each unit with a focus question that dealt with a universal issue and asked students to think beyond a specific event. For example, when dealing with the concept of conflict and the Civil War, we asked, "Why do some conflicts escalate to violence?" At the same time, we realized that historical knowledge was vital to understand such a question. What about the story and the chronology of the events? We sought to handle this concern by sequencing the concepts chronologically. That meant we examined freedom and authority using the American Revolution and constitutional period before we taught conflict and conflict management using the Civil War and Reconstruction.

The three of us were committed to one more central element in the course—the importance of teaching critical-thinking skills. We called them inquiry skills, and we relied on Edwin Fenton, Jack Fraenkel, and Hilda Taba for much of our thinking. We started each unit with a high-level question that would become the focus for our inquiry in class. We might show a film, do a role-play, or read an original document and ask students to develop hypotheses on the question, given the limited amount of information available. We proceeded to test the validity of these hypotheses as we encountered the historical data in the unit. As the data increased, we categorized them conceptually, finally asking students to write a generalization in response to the focus question. The units did not conclude with objective tests but with three-page essays on the focus question.

We soon realized that the course we had written did not work for some students. The initial course, because it had been financed by gifted funds, was designed for "Honors" level students, of which El Cerrito High School had a sizable minority. However, the school population of El Cerrito was gradually changing and becoming more diverse. Under the district's integration plan, many black students from the city of Richmond were enrolling at El Cerrito.

A significant Asian population was moving into the city. The Bay Area was a mecca for new immigrants, particularly from Taiwan, Hong Kong, Vietnam, and Korea. The white population, mostly from the hills of Kensington and El Cerrito and often connected with the University of California at Berkeley, continued to come, although they were no longer the dominant majority. As a department, we now faced many more students who were deficient in reading and language skills and unprepared for the rigors of the American Experience course.

Coping with Needs of a Changing Student Population

Our next summer session was devoted to the educational needs of the changing student population. What we created was a second American Experience course, based on the same philosophy as the first, but delivered in an entirely different way. We retained the conceptual-chronological units but limited each one to two weeks. The two-week pattern was standard for each unit; we opened with a high interest motivator to grab students' attention (in fact, we called these lessons grabbers). Next, we spent a day introducing and practicing the skill objective of the unit. We ended the first week with two days of individualized instruction where students chose to do three or four assignments from a list of eight to ten, each one designed to understand the concept, the history, or the skill. We called these days "Option Days" because of the choices involved. These days became very effective; students worked very hard, and we were able to circulate among them giving needed individual help. There were also drawbacks; some students never fully understood the central idea of some of the options; the output did not always equal the input involved in creating the option. Yet given the diversity of the students, we agreed that some type of individualized program was important.

The second week focused on an activity in which students applied what they learned during week one. These weeks often included debates or role-plays in which students became newly arriving immigrants or labor leaders. The unit concluded with a test of the concept, content, and skill on the final day. The two-week pattern reflected our belief that these students needed the structure, regularity, and closure it provided. Yet the pattern did not destroy the conceptual foundation of the initial course nor did it prevent us from using the activities that gave the course its energy.

Students found American Experience challenging, confusing, and often exciting. Most found the course difficult because it required more than rote memory. Many had come from history classes that only required answering recall questions. Often in the middle of categorizing or at the end of a discussion, I asked whether they were confused. If they were, I praised them, assuring them that a high level of uncertainty was often the sign of thinking that had penetrated beneath what was obvious. My response was of no comfort at the time, but I knew they understood what I was saying and agreed.

Despite the confusion and the challenge (or perhaps because of it) students were often excited by the class, particularly by the activities. On debate or mock-trial days, energy was high—they entered and left the room talking about what was happening. I asked some students whether my impressions were correct. One senior, Carlos Martin, said: "One of the things I most enjoyed about my American Experience class was the openness. The topics brought up allowed us to say anything that was on our minds. And with the whole class opening their mouths, I opened my mind to the class's diversity in ideas and people. It was a firsthand view of America's history and, probably more important, history-in-the-making."

Some Illustrations

An examination of a single unit can illustrate many of these ideas. For this purpose, I have chosen the unit that opens American Experience, the one that focuses on freedom and authority. I have chosen it because it contains most of the elements I have outlined, yet it has undergone significant change since its inception.

The initial course began with units on the nature of man, American values using a colonial setting, and revolution using the War for Independence and American constitutionalism. The unit on the nature of man started with the question: What is the nature of man, and how is it reflected in his choice of government? Students read excerpts from great Western philosophers, including Aristotle, Thomas Hobbes, John Locke, John Stuart Mill, Thomas Jefferson, and Emma Goldman. Reading and discussing these philosophers was tremendously exciting because the students had never been exposed to the actual words of so many scholars writing about such fundmental issues. In the early 1970s, it was easy to find students willing to defend Emma Goldman's call for anarchy. Today, it is harder but I'm always amazed by the willingness of adolescents to play the game and adapt to the requests of the teacher.

As teachers, we tried to be as Socratic as possible—accepting but challenging all ideas, answering questions with questions. Anyone who is experienced at classroom questioning knows how demanding that style can be. I struggle with it even today after 20 years, trying to find the patience to wait, trying to listen to each response closely so my next question is framed by the student's response. That kind of patience and concentration required for inquiry teaching may have forced many a teacher who tried inquiry methods to abandon them.

As the nature-of-man unit evolved, we felt it lacked diversity of materials. Most of the unit was discussion based on original sources. We found two films that added a visual dimension—one an excellent dramatization called *Machiavelli: Man and the State,* and the second a humorous and provocative series of espisodes called *Why Man Creates.* Still, the unit needed an activity. Luckily at a workshop, sponsored by the California Council for the Social Studies, I found the perfect simulation game, deceptively labeled "Cooperation." The game divides the class into six groups, each one asked to decide whether to vote "X" or "Y" in 10 separate rounds. The "X" and "Y" have no meaning beyond the rewards and penalties assigned to each group depending on the way they vote. It presents students with the question whether they can trust their neighbor, whether you should protect your self-interest or stay true to your principles and ideals. It is a fine example of how simulation and role-playing can vividly illustrate and clarify what others have been writing about. We had our Machiavellis and Goldmans right there in class.

The additions to the unit certainly enhanced it with a diversity it lacked before. However, strong units never remain static. Our district sponsored a series of workshops taught by a Southern California group concerned with law-related education, Law in a Free Society. Their workshop suggested that we could extend our nature-of-man-and-government ideas by combining them with our study of the American Revolution and the constitutional period if we used one of their basic concepts—freedom and authority. The materials created by Law in a Free Society posed four questions that we chose as the orientation for a new unit called Freedom and Authority that would combine the philosophy from the nature-of-man unit, the history of the American Revolution, and governmental principles underlining the creation of the Consitution. Here are the questions:[2]

- What is authority? What is freedom?
- What are the sources of authority and freedom?
- What are the costs and benefits of authority and freedom?
- What should be the scope and limits of authority and freedom?

These questions became the framework for the discussion of the ideas of the different philosophers.

Clearly what we have created is a dynamic, ever-changing course wherein few units are now taught as originally planned. That may be one of the secrets of its success. It happens because the team enjoys what we teach, and we enjoy one another. But we pay a price. Constant revision means scores of planning meetings after school, often lasting until dark. In the early years, we often did that two or three days a week throughout the school year. It is far more difficult now that California has lengthened the school day and school does not end until 3:30 P.M. The result is that we have become less willing to challenge what we might like to change and are more ready "to do it the way we did it last year." Yet we all know that it is constant revision that keeps us young in the classroom.

Revising the American Revolution Unit

Revising the American Revolution unit around the freedom-and-authority question gave it new meaning. We had previously taught the unit around the question, Why does man revolt? I was never entirely happy with that question, since some students had already dealt with that issue when they studied the French Revolution in the 9th grade. In addition, Daniel Boorstin and other historians have persuasively argued that the American Revolution was not a revolution at all.[3]

The new focus became: When does someone have the right to challenge authority? We wanted to open the new unit with a grabber that would allow students to understand the conflict between freedom and authority from a personal perspective. We chose to use a moral dilemma strategy using Rosa Parks' decision not to move to the back of the bus.[4] Although unrelated to the American Revolution, Parks' dilemma was similar to those faced by some rebels who took up arms against their mother country. I have always had a good student response to moral dilemma strategies. I realize that research on whether or not they raise one's level of moral reasoning is inconclusive. However, the dilemmas always raise important questions and stimulate significant discussion.

The centerpiece of the unit is a debate on the question, Did the British Parliament have legitimate authority to tax the American colonies? The question asks students to look at the scope, limits, and sources of authority. What makes the debate unique is the format. After opening speeches by each side, the debate is turned over to teams of interrogators (the rebels vs. the loyalists) who question each other. At any time during the interrogation, one side may shout "CREAM" indicating that they think they deserve points for the quality of their questions and answers or the failure of their opposition to respond effectively. A panel of students judges whether points for the "cream" should be granted. Finally (two days later), each side presents a closing speech, and the jury of students announces the winner. The competitive edge encouraged by this debate style stimulates student interest and involvement and improves the depth of research. And the word 'cream' is heard softly from various parts of the room for the rest of the year.

We give the various teams of interrogators (usually one is the spokesperson and the other a research assistant) a couple of days in class to search for good questions, arguments, and evidence. The primary sources are original documents from the prerevolutionary period—a speech to Parliament by Prime Minister Grenville, Benjamin Franklin's testimony before British legislators, Soame Jenyn's article on virtual representation. The use of original documents allows students to use the data to form their own interpretations, unfiltered by the purposes of a textbook author. This is not to say that we have rejected the textbook altogether. Each student has one (Thomas Bailey's *The American Pageant*)[5] and is tested periodically on assigned chapters. However, we use a textbook much as we would an encyclopedia—we send students to it for information relevant to class activities, such as the debate.

The Textbook Issue

The textbook issue presented us with a fundamental educational question: To what extent are we responsible for teaching a factual narrative history of the United States? At the beginning of American Experience, we did not hold students responsible for reading the narrative except as they might use it for a debate or mock trial. A great deal of history was taught, but we never measured how much they knew. Ten years later, we concluded that our students knew less history than before. Perhaps they wrote better, thought more critically, or liked history more, but they certainly were not reading the text carefully. At that point, we began to assign chapters to read with periodic multiple-choice tests. The reading was to be done entirely outside class with little class time spent on its explanation. We have since replaced the multiple-choice tests with a series of terms or persons to identify and have coordinated the reading more closely with the in-class activities. What we have produced is a sensible compromise—our students should improve their level of historical literacy if they remember what they have read, and we have not become slaves to the textbook.

In addition to the classroom debate and the outside text reading, we want students to be exposed to historical interpretation. A central goal of the course is for students to discover that history is interpretation, filtered by the lens of the historian. In this unit we ask students to read an excerpt from Louis Hacker on the economic origins of the Revolution. Given the difficulty of such college level material, we conduct one day of small group seminars where students do some peer teaching to clarify questions they have about the reading. The students find the readings and seminars challenging, but there is excellent interaction and questioning during these sessions. Their minds are definitely awake.

At the close of the unit on the Revolution, it is time to integrate all that the students have learned into some type of meaningful package. In American Experience, this package is often a three-page essay requiring a series of critical-thinking skills. We have labeled it an inquiry essay, and it is the central writing assignment of the course. It begins with the question in the case of this unit, How did political ideas combine with economic interests to produce the American Revolution? In their essays, students are asked to begin with a generalization in response to the question and analyze the generalization by examining how each component part fits into the generalization and how the evidence supports it. Developing such a generalization requires a discipline most students have not faced. They are required to place all the evidence collected during the debate into categories and label each category. From the labels, they are required to develop a series of cause-effect relationships which form the basis for the generalization. Once the generalization is ready, they can return to the evidence and examine how it supports it, concluding with either a restatement or revision of their initial thesis. The process is rooted in Hilda Taba's work and teaches a series of critical-thinking skills.[6]

The Writing Problems

Some students resist the process because of its discipline. They question its purpose. They prefer to write their opinions or their "impressions." They resist the demand for detail and historical fact. Other students are simply confused because there is no right or wrong answer. But what is produced by the student who follows the process and struggles with it can be highly creative and insightful. One of the best examples is this generalization written by Lynne Bui last year on what explains the success of the U.S. Constitution:

> The United States Constitution is acknowledged throughout the world today not only because of its longevity but also because of its contribution to modern government. It has endured two centuries of changing times, needs, and circumstances; it will continue to stand for centuries more. Perhaps it can be said that when a constitutional government, based on compromise between authority and liberty, establishes a balance within itself, thus providing for stability inside the political systems, and allows for its own flexibility to fit the changing needs, it has not only satisfied man's two conflicting natures but also established nationwide uniformity.

Such writing is rewarding for both teacher and student. Bonnie Taylor, a member of the American Experience staff, has often felt those rewards: "Teachers need a good pat on the back. It is always pleasing when students return from the universities and tell us that our course taught them to think and write in a way that they can really use." Students also appreciate the inquiry process, which asks them to go beyond the mere memorization of historical fact. Phoebe Schroeder, who is finishing her third semester of American Experience, now expresses this idea: "I learned more than dates, names, and places in American Experience. I learned process. I understood the method of history. And that knowledge will stay with me far past graduation. Just like the title of the course—American Experience. Not history, experience. That's exactly what it is, experiencing history."

We spend a couple of days illustrating each constitutional principle. My favorite set of lessons is an advocate decision-making activity that illustrates checks and balances. Advocate decision-making is a form of individualized debate that I first encountered in one of Clair Keller's sessions at the 1973 NCSS meeting in San Francisco.[7] The strategy is perfect for any contemporary or historical controversy. It begins with a clarification of the issue for debate—in the case of checks and balances, it is whether or not Franklin Roosevelt should have packed the Supreme Court after they overturned the Agricultural Adjustment Act and the National Industrial Recovery Act in the 1930s.

Reflections on the Experience

What I have presented here is not a prescription for success in the social studies classroom. It is one department's experience, unique to their personalities and background and made possible by a diverse and talented group of kids. It is successful because it grew from the bottom upward with only minimal interference from the top. It grew because of a group of teachers who had a sense of purpose and mission that superseded their own selfish interests. It grew because of team planning that allowed a diversity of ideas to weave a stronger, more creative product. It grew because we genuinely liked the subject we taught. It grew because students, despite all the stresses in the adolescent world, want to discover the excitement and thrill of learning.

Certainly developing rational and humane citizens is what social studies education is all about. In response to my request to state what he liked most about the American Experience course he has taught, my colleague, Bruce Greene, replied: "American Experience is a highly participatory course; as such, it ensures that students will learn and propagate a strong sense of the democratic process." Bruce is right. Participation is central—for teachers as well as students—teachers interacting with fellow teachers and students interacting with fellow students. Without it, the sense of inadequacy, alienation, and bitterness among teachers will grow. Without it, the sense of political distrust, inefficacy, and alienation found among adolescents will continue. Open minds, interaction, and the exchange of ideas in the teacher's workroom as well as the classroom have been the road to effective education and democratic citizenship.

Notes

[1]Social Sciences Education Framework Committee, *Social Sciences Education Framework for California Public Schools* (Sacramento: California State Department of Education, 1968).

[2]Law in a Free Society, *Authority* (Santa Monica: Law in a Free Society, 1977).

[3]Daniel Boorstin, *Genius of American Politics* (Chicago: University of Chicago Press, 1962).

[4]Nona Lyons, Guest Editor, "Four People Who Made Choices," *Social Education* 38 (February 1974):134.

[5]Thomas Bailey and David Kennedy, *The American Pageant* (Lexington, Massachusetts: D.C. Heath, 1983).

[6]Hilda Taba, *Teaching Handbook for Elementary Social Studies* (Reading, Massachusetts: Addison-Wesley, 1967).

[7]Clair Keller, An Advocate/Decision-making Activity on Alternative Uses of Public Land, NCSS Annual Meeting, November 23, 1973.

CHAPTER 10

SOCIOLOGY AND SOCIAL RESEARCH:

A RURAL-URBAN EXCHANGE

Pauline U. Dyson

One of the challenges in teaching any social studies course, especially one that deals with the behavioral sciences, is to have students understand why the subject is important. Why is human behavior worthy of investigation? Why should anyone bother to find out, beyond mere personal experience, about relationships between people, about prejudice, about love and hate, about heredity and environment, and about family? These are some of the large social issues often included in a high school sociology course. On one level, they may be topics vaguely familiar to students, yet as academic subjects beyond their personal applications, they are frequently unfamiliar. Often what is new is that these topics are actually studied and investigated in a systematic way by social scientists.

Indeed, it seems curious to many adolescents that people exist who earn their living studying the behavior of people in the past (social historians), or of people in diverse cultures (anthropologists), or of social grouping today (sociologists), or of interpersonal behaviors (psychologists). What do these social scientists do that is the same as or different from the rest of society in learning about people? Why are they paid for making observations, for teaching, and for writing articles and books? Is not most human behavior explained by common sense anyway?

The Scientific Method

Teachers confront this initial reaction to the behavioral social sciences as they introduce students to the scientific method of investigation. Students usually seem familiar with the steps that social scientists go through to arrive at their conclusions, as they have learned them from courses in biology or chemistry:

1. What do you want to know about this subject? Have a question worth investigating.
2. From previous research and existing theory, develop a hypothesis.
3. What information will be needed to test the hypothesis, how will the data be collected and analyzed?
4. Gather the data. Process and classify the information to test the hypothesis.

5. The hypothesis is reexamined in light of the research. What was substantiated, what was rejected, what was changed? What new learning takes place?

The differences between the physical and social sciences are acknowledged by students who understand that it is not possible to "put people under a microscope." They recognize the unpredictability of the human behavior with its resistance to being weighed, measured, and analyzed by social scientists.

What is more difficult for high school students to understand is the actual process of social science investigation. For years, teachers have used the inquiry approach as part of their teaching strategies, but far too often they themselves are in control of its implementation. Students are the recipients of the planned stage-by-stage development from hypothesis to thesis, but they are rarely in charge of directing the learning themselves. That is, in American classrooms, the scientific or inquiry method is a tool of teaching, though less frequently, a tool for learning.

Investigation in the Social Sciences

If students are to understand more fully what social scientists do and what scientific method is all about, it is essential that they have practice as amateur social scientists in conducting their own empirical investigations. Furthermore, the question or problem to be investigated should be one that students themselves recognize as important or relevant, not one that is assigned by the teacher or textbook.

This does not preclude the teacher's creating an interest in various topics, perhaps in subject areas a student had not thought much about before. Here the teacher must be sensitive to students' individual responses to topics introduced. If sharing of ideas is encouraged in the classroom from the beginning, students will not shy away from being very direct about what piques their interest and what does not.

Any problem that students themselves identify as meaningful is usually one that carries with it personal interpretations, preconceptions, and biases. Sometimes emotional reactions to complex societal problems are so strong in adolescence that adopting the necessary rational, objective approach is difficult. This tension between social science methodology and the difficulties of its application and presentation is what challenges the high school teacher.

This challenge was to be met in an elective sociology class of 11th and 12th graders. I soon learned that the topic of religion, which interested their counterparts a decade ago, had lost its appeal. Rather than trying to force an interest in the sociological phenomena of modern religious development, I continued to explore the possibilities of other topics with the students. Three of these met an immediate acceptance—sibling relationships, the changing nature of childhood, and the black family in today's world.

Subjects Considered

The first two subjects, siblings and childhood, were heavily favored by students largely because of their personal identification with the topics. The third topic was less familiar to students in the white, middle-class, rural-suburban small town where I teach. They had virtually no experience with the dynamics and problems of black family life. In spite of the usual stereotypes that students of their experience possess, the subject of the black family was relatively new and not directly personal. It thus provided a perfect opportunity to employ the sociological scientific method premised, as it is, on objectivity and dispassion.

Despite their lack of familiarity with the subject, student interest was keen once I had laid the groundwork with materials to stimulate their curiosity. The class watched the television documentary on the black family with Bill Moyers, in which inner-city teenage mothers and fathers expressed honestly their feelings about parenthood, sex, responsibility, welfare, and male/female roles in ghetto life. The immediate reaction of my white, middle-class students was how far removed the young people in the television show seemed, in values and upbringing, from their own circumstances. Students wondered, Why is a poor fifteen-year-old mother proud of having a baby, when I "would die" if I ever became pregnant? How can the absent father of the baby be proud, but not feel an obligation to take responsibility to support the child? Why is using contraceptives regarded as "unmanly" by some black young men? Is there a close relationship (the term 'female bonding' is introduced) between the teenage mothers and their own mothers that is different from the normal mother-daughter relationship?

Students were convinced that this television program showed a world as different from their own in culture and values as any foreign, Third World society they knew of. The question of what accounts for the sharp difference among teenagers, living in a small country, was inescapable. Why were there so many differences between young people living in a rural community and those of large cities within the same country?

Other questions followed. How representative was the program of black inner-city life? How accurate was it? Was Moyers overemphasizing "differences" in values? With so many varied and diverse questions, research topics emerged rather easily. Here step one of the scientific method described above was coming into focus. Students wanted to find out more by visiting and talking with students in an inner-city school. Could they visit their school to see what is was like? Step three in the scientific method was now being addressed. How could we acquire data to answer our questions apart from the usual printed materials available in library sources? As teacher-guide through this learning process, I welcomed the students' desire to do original research. This is the stuff of which sociologists are made.

Dealing with Student Sensitivities

My enthusiasm for the students' interest and commitment was initially tempered with personal concerns. How would inner-city blacks feel about being studied? Was our desire to visit an inner-city school a rebirth of what black leaders condemned as "slumming" 20 years ago? Would our interest in serious learning, however genuine and innocent, lead to misunderstanding, perhaps even to solidifying bias and stereotypes among blacks and whites? I weighed the risks and concluded that potential gains in understanding by both groups justified the effort.

Through a professional acquaintance, I was able to arrange a trip to Hartford High School, an inner-city high school where a social studies teacher expressed interest in an exchange visit. He, too, shared the idea that there is much to be learned when young people from diverse racial and socioeconomic backgrounds meet one to one. His proposal was to bring academically talented, economically underprivileged students to our rural-suburban school district to discover what differences and similarities existed between the "two worlds." Though we both recognized the risk that the activity might result in reinforcing stereotypes on both sides, our faith in the students' ability to learn and in their capacity for open-minded objectivity led us to press forward. The teacher's enthusiasm matched my own and helped ease my concerns.

We made arrangements for the exchange. Students from both high schools were enthusiastic, excited, and yet fearful in anticipation. The high school we were to visit had received good press for its no-nonsense administration and renewed emphasis on academic achievement. Still, the stereotype of "inner-city" gave some of my students pause, reflecting perhaps a latent racism that most of us experience when races are separated by social class economics and geography.

While arrangements were being made and preparatory discussions held, students continued their study of the black experience by reading that classic of many sociology classes, *Manchild in a Promised Land,* by Claude Brown. Unlike many books about the black experience published and taught in American high schools in the 1960s and 1970s, this book has not lost its timelessness or pertinence in the 1980s. Perhaps this is because Claude Brown writes in the first person, the poignant voice of a child growing up in Harlem. No matter how diverse the growing-up experience is, the feelings of the main character, his need for love, caring, and attention are not different from those of any students. Students detected this universality of emotion, all the while reacting with shock at the everyday experiences of Brown in a world where stealing and skipping school were accepted events.

These realizations made it possible for me to focus student thinking on the effect of environment on making us who we are. Somehow the rather abstract sociological notions about environment vs. heredity, language, and socialization that we had been studying all year became meaningful as we tackled the questions of what formed Claude Brown. How was he able to overcome these material, spiritual, and emotional hardships when so many of his friends could not? Was it something innate, such as basic intelligence? Was it determination, character, or influences of family and friends that accounted for his ability to overcome the depressing, drug- and crime-ridden life of Harlem? Students had differing answers to these questions as brought out in discussions and essays.

Several students hypothesized that the drug culture—particularly heroin and crack—was not as pervasive in the Harlem of the 1950s as it is today. Perhaps Claude Brown's Harlem offered more choices and opportunities for "success" as measured by middle-class norms. Others extended this thesis, citing the Moyers film and posited that the drug culture has much to do with the attitudes and values of today's minorities. They wondered if they would see drug dealing going on in the inner-school we were to visit. At the very least, students anticipated seeing crack, the drug about which they had read so much in recent newspaper reports.

Personal Identification with Other People

Students had become so involved with the person of Claude Brown that they were excited to learn that I had recorded a television program, *Harlem Revisited,* done by Brown himself. In this program, Brown goes back to the Harlem of his youth to see how it had changed. He found an increase in street violence and armed robberies, an effect of the easy availability of handguns. Although poverty had always existed in Harlem, criminal activity had increased markedly. The program focused on the prevalence of drugs that served as an escape from the hopelessness of ghetto living for many Harlemites. Would a modern-day Claude Brown escape, the students wondered, given the worsening conditions in many inner cities?

At this point, the students spontaneously decided to write a class letter to Claude Brown to ask whether they could interview him. Through the aid of the librarian who located an address, and with all the students contributing ideas, the letter was finally composed and mailed. Unfortunately, they received no response. The realities of step four—gathering data—hit home. The students learned that, in researching a topic, one encounters dead ends—difficulties that force sociologists to try alternative methods of getting information.

Perhaps that field trip to an urban high school would be an alternative way of finding out about the experiences of black youth. It was clear that the teachers and students at Hartford High School were receptive to our plans for the student exchange. At first we exchanged information about the size, student populations, and community setting of our respective schools.

Student Fears and Expectations

It was only when we planned for the visit that would involve having a buddy system—a Hartford High student paired with a Coginchaug student—for the day's exchange that certain latent fears began to appear. Students' biases of what inner-city kids are like came through clearly as they recorded their previsit expectations.

Among these expectations were: "I will be only one of a few white faces walking through the halls. That is frightening." "I imagine the school dirty and the walls covered with obscene graffiti." "There will be many pregnant students in classes." "Somebody is sure to approach me to buy drugs." "I wonder if I can understand my partners if they speak Spanish or Black English." "The school will have lots of tall basketball players." "Their classes will surely be easy compared to ours." (These questions could be the hypothesis stage of the scientific method as we observed.)

I asked students to save these impressions and compare them with their observations and impressions gained during the visit. Were their assumptions valid? Did they correspond with what other students saw or witnessed? Is there a way of accounting for discrepancies, or was there enough evidence to prove or disprove a hypothesis? Were their perceptions prejudiced? What is prejudice or bias anyway? Were their perceptions gained by studying *Manchild in a Promised Land* or by watching the documentary on black America? Were they formed by things they had seen or read in the past? Was there a sense that the values assumed by a white, middle-class culture such as ours were somehow better than or superior to the values of inner-city people?

At this point, it was crucial to stress the importance of objectivity as a goal. Students came to realize that some of their hunches might prove wrong, others correct, and still other left undecided. It was essential to point out the steps or stages of the scientific method that one was following as students went through them in a relatively unconscious way. This exercise set forth the basis for our research with its simple attempt to get at the premises of our assumptions and then to find out how to test them against a real experience. It is important to note the point of social science research we were on at each stage of our investigation.

Preparations for the Exercise

A similar, though more informal, exercise was conducted at Hartford High School in preparation for their visit to our school. Discussions revealed many latent fears about white, rural-suburban high schools. Some urban students hold the preppy subgroup in derision. Even the rural setting outside the city seems uncontrolled and overwhelming to youngsters who are more comfortable in streets and neighborhoods. Many of these students had never been out of the city of Hartford, so a forty-mile trip to the "boonies" was in itself an adventure. They wondered if they might get lost in the wilds of the countryside. Would they see more animals—cows, chickens—than people? Could they understand one another when they talked? Would the white students be "uppity" or friendly? Would they all be tall, blond, athletic-looking, and preppy? Would the Hartford students feel out-of-place and "put down" among rich students sporting designer clothes?

After the first awkward moments of pairing took place, the students went off with their partners following the host student's class schedule for the day. It was interesting that when the students were first introduced to one another, their names (some very ethnic—Hispanic or Asian, others very Anglo) seemed hard to pronounce and remember. Strangeness in names seemed only to reconfirm anticipated notions of differences between the two groups. It was not long, however, before the students began to know one another, to talk about things that are the cachet of teenage experience no matter what the existing cultural chasm—sports, classes, boyfriends/girlfriends, dreams, and plans for the future. From their exchanges, awkward at first but increasingly understanding, friendships emerged. Each student, whether urban or rural/suburban became more open as the day progressed, chatting, giggling, and groaning in typical adolescent fashion. Students began to drop their initial fears of one another and enjoy the similarities and diversities of their lives.

What and How We Learned

After the visit, we analyzed the exchange experience. Did we lose or gain objectivity assessing the diversity of another high school, as we got to know the other students? Do social scientists have to maintain a dispassionate attitude throughout their research in order to view and record data that are scientifically valid? Are we, as high school students, different from social scientists? Are there other needs that we were addressing in this experiment besides the formal one of gathering evidence to support or refute hypotheses concerning inner-city youth and black family life? Discussion of these questions highlighted both problems and potential of the scientific method as applied to sociology.

Both during and after the visits, evidence was gathered, impressions were shared, and the questions we had at the start of the experiment were raised again. Original hypotheses, using scientific method, were tested against the evidence. What did we learn about the values of inner-city youngsters, their family lives, the problems of pregnant teenagers and young motherhood, the effects of drugs, and the roles of males/females in ghetto life? How close were the experiences of the people interviewed in Bill Moyers' documentary and Claude Brown's book to what we saw and discussed with our urban counterparts? How did our hypotheses and prejudgments about city life hold up in the light of our research?

Students were asked to write about each of the expectations they had had before the visits to see what reinforcements, modifications, and outright rejections resulted from the exchange. What follows are some of the revised judgments stated in terms of actual learnings or conclusions made by the students themselves.

On Teenage Pregnancy and Motherhood. Although there were not many visibly pregnant girls walking around Hartford High, students were startled to learn how casually students talked of their friends who have had babies or of students absent to care for a sick child at home. Social condemnation of having babies while still a teenager and unmarried seemed absent from the city school.

On School Parents. Most urban students visiting our school said that they did not expect their parents to visit their school on parents' night to discuss their grades. In contrast, slightly over half the parents at our rural/suburban high school had come the evening before for the purpose of discussing student progress with the teaching staff. When asked why their parents seemed uninterested, the city youngsters answered that their mothers and fathers felt uncomfortable and sometimes embarrassed talking to teachers. The sociology students concluded that the school and education are middle-class institutions that reflect the values of that social class. They began to understand why inner-city students do not naturally take to the goals and objectives of school life. They reflected on their own advantage in having a common set of values, those fostered by the school as well as their parents.

On Sports, School Activities. Our students, who literally expected to see black students dribbling a basketball through the halls of Hartford High, were surprised to find that few students had turned out for the "come out for basketball" recruitment night. Instead, teachers were seen approaching students in the hall to tell them about coming out for the sport or reminding them about a practice session after school. Indeed, the teacher from Hartford High who was instrumental in arranging this exchange, was the football coach who had to tutor students so that there would be enough academically eligible players (C or above in courses) to make the team. Student activities that take up so much of our students' interests and time seemed not to be of such concern to the Hartford students who had to work at home or in a job after school.

On Courses, Learning, Academics. A few students noted some city high school courses dealing with topics more typically studied in suburban middle school curricula. Others found subjects and instruction equally challenging. One thing they noticed was that some top academic students had courses with a practical, vocational slant. Rather than studying economics as such, students learned about business, its procedures, marketing, and advertising. There seemed to be a stress on obtaining marketable skills, even though the students would generally go on to four-year colleges.

On Drugs, Graffiti, "Tough Types." Students were amazed to find that the drug problem had decreased in this inner-city high school as it seems to have in many suburban schools. Alcohol was cited as the number one abused substance, which corresponds to the situation in suburban high schools as well. There may be drugs such as crack, coke, and pot on the streets of Hartford, and some high school students may be involved with them, but there was virtually no observable buying, selling, or use on campus. This was due partly to the vigilance of the teachers and administrators who have set up tough school rules on substance use. Besides, more students seemed to condemn the use of drugs and alcohol in the school environment. The graffiti-filled halls, especially the lavatories, which my students expected as part of the urban high school scene, proved not to be the case. Although there was some writing on lavatory walls, it was no more nor less obscene than that found in our own high school. As for the much feared "tough types," student prejudgments again proved wrong. For the most part, the students appeared friendly, wholesome, and well-dressed. There were fewer of the preppy-dressed students, whereas there were also fewer of the "punk" style than appear in the halls of our rural-suburban high school.

Evaluating the Process
What did we learn from all this? Although not all the questions we started with were answered, students gained insight into a subject of concern to modern sociologists and students of current affairs while practicing procedures of scientific method within the perimeters of the high school setting.

In addition, they discovered that comparative cultural studies can take place within a few miles of their own communities. They came to understand that human behavior itself is interesting and worthy of serious study. It is essential that we compare impressions gained from life itself or from books, television programs, and films with the reality of what is there waiting to be discovered.

Students learned to refrain from making hasty judgments and from forming facile opinions. One needs to test hunches and hypotheses against accumulated data. With an exchange program as a vehicle, students discovered that presumptions or prejudices can obscure the truth unless tested by experimentation and observation.

This experience took us beyond the academic discipline and its application of the scientific method. There is a difference between theory and reality. Our prejudices often blind us from comprehension. Mutual human understanding can only be fostered and ignorance avoided by finding out for oneself.

Our student project could be interpreted as insensitive, naive, and dangerous. Some might object to seeking to maintain objectivity or dispassion in any study of the inner city. Objectivity in the face of what many call injustice may seem cruel and insensitive. The experience of students, both as sociologists and as members of the human family, can lead to naive statements, half-formed impressions and, in the worst case, misunderstanding and misinformation. It is impossible for a teacher or the class to correct errors, challenge all racist attitudes, and impose a "tolerant" understanding view. Given these limitations, our project could have been dangerous, contributing to stereotypes rather than beginning a long process of opening minds and changing attitudes.

These challenges raise important questions. What are the social studies if they are not about understanding real and significant issues, and not just the safe ones? What are the social studies if they are not about seeking accurate information without prejudicing the outcome? What are the social studies if they are not about student participation in real learning? And what are the social studies if they are not about long-term learning of attitudes and values? Our project did not solve the race problem nor did it enable white students to understand the black experience or the inner-city experience, but it opened windows on learning about sociological research and learning about our own prejudices and what it means to be human. It was worth the risk.

REFERENCES

Brown, Claude. *Manchild in the Promised Land.* New York: Macmillan, 1965.
Moyers, Bill. *The Vanishing Family,* television special on the problem of black families in America.

CHAPTER 11

TEACHING ECONOMICS IN THE INFORMATION AGE:

CHALLENGES AND OPPORTUNITIES

John Driscoll

What a great time to be teaching social studies! We are at the threshold of a Technological Revolution—an Information Age. Disorder swirls around us. Each new crisis simultaneously frightens and exhilarates. It is as if there existed an energy-level ratchet; each shock moves society up another notch. All this disorder, together with the intense energy it generates, finds its way into our classrooms.

If the evidence accumulated thus far points to any trend, it is that contradictions and paradox will be dominant characteristics of the Information Age. Perhaps the two greatest paradoxes relate to technology and information themselves. Technological development promises a higher standard of living. Yet there is a pervasive feeling that the quality of life is declining. Access to information is a precondition of being informed. Yet it seems as if the quantity of information is a barrier to being informed.

The explanation of both these apparent paradoxes lies in the fact that our ability to develop technology and produce information far exceeds our ability to manage applications of technology and to process vast quantities of information. Technology seems to threaten our environment and, more significantly, our human spirit. The creation of information, rather than informing, leads to a condition that Charles White (1987) calls infoglut. Our institutions are groaning under the weight of these emerging realities.

A recognition of these realities has provided a focus for educational reform, and the energy generated by the disorder of the Information Age has fueled this reform movement. The substance of early reactionary back-to-basics demands has recently been changed and enhanced by the work of the Carnegie Task Force on Teaching as a Profession (1986), the National Endowment for the Humanities (1987), E. D. Hirsch, Jr. (1987), and Allan Bloom (1987). In each of these cases, the authors have argued for deeper commitment to transmitting cultural knowledge so that citizens will have the contextual base required to filter and analyze information, skills that are necessary in making informed choices. Coincident with the shift away from the initial back-to-basics theme has come a movement to reestablish the social studies as a central component of school curriculum, a change that stands in stark contrast to the mathematics/ science orientation of the first wave of reform efforts.

The Need for Technological Literacy

One immediate result of this shift in emphasis to the social studies is a requirement that teachers become technologically literate. Technological literacy implies not only a degree of comfort with technology, but also an understanding of the effect that technology has on society. Linton Deck, a former superintendent of Fairfax County, Virginia, schools, called educators who were unwilling to accept this responsibility techno-peasants. I believe this appellation irritated a number of teachers partly because they sensed that the underlying message was true. Quite simply, technologically illiterate social studies teachers are incapable of serving students in the Information Age.

Technological literacy is an example of the special burdens that the Information Age places on teachers and others who work with the social studies curriculum. The challenges to all who design, develop, and implement curriculum can be traced to at least two other sources. First, as suggested earlier, is content. A second set of challenges arises from the type of student produced by today's culture.

The content debate between advocates of core curriculum and those who argue for a current-issues approach has escalated recently. It appears that there is a stunning contrast in cultural and geographic knowledge between today's students and those of a generation ago. The proposed remedy that emphasizes teaching long lists of names, dates, and places, however, seems intuitively wrongheaded. In any event, this debate has caused, in the words of David King (1987),

> continuing confusion about what should be taught, how, and for what reason. Thus, social studies educators on different levels have an additional problem; while having to cope with a ready-fire-aim world, they cannot agree on where the bull's-eye is or even where the target is.

This passionate debate over content has a tendency to obscure considerations about the students we face in our classrooms. Today's student, pulled in a substantial number of directions, is distracted from schooling. Part-time work during the school year is just one example. I teach in Fairfax County, Virginia, a relatively wealthy jurisdiction in suburban Washington, D.C. The average family income in my school's community approaches six figures. Yet, a surprising number of my senior government and economics students work during the school year. The cost of working is time from homework and school-based extracurricular activities and less attentiveness in class. School cannot be a center of life for someone who works 15 to 30 hours each week.

Coping with Student Indifference

Student indifference to learning, always a frustration to teachers, has recently become almost disheartening. It has exacerbated the difficulty of finding appropriate methods through which curriculum can be delivered effectively. For both these reasons, I am particularly encouraged about a course developed by Junior Achievement Inc.—Applied Economics.

I am fascinated by economics for two reasons. First, the discipline of economics provides a useful structure for critical thinking. Second, an understanding of economics content is essential to effective citizenship.

A wag once described what happened when an economist was stranded on an island—"he assumed a can of beans." What better skill for a citizen to possess, however, than the compulsion to specify the premises or assumptions upon which arguments rest? This, to me, is the fundamental structural component of critical thinking. I particularly remember one of my economics students who came late to class, carrying a cup that showed the logo of an off-campus hamburger stand. I reminded her of the rule that forbids leaving school grounds. Her retort was instantaneous; "What are your assumptions?" I told her that I could see the cup. "Aha!" she cried, "And what would happen if you changed your assumptions? Would I be in as much trouble if my friend got this for me?"

What Can the Social Studies Offer?

In this simple anecdote about classroom banter is embedded the essence of what the social studies have to offer. The anecdote demonstrates a young person's nascent ability to think productively. It is immensely rewarding to me when one of my students applies this skill outside an economics paradigm, even if it is at my expense.

When I think about economics content, I am always drawn to the observation on the subject Thomas Carlyle made after reading Malthus. "Economics," he said, "is the dismal science." It is certainly true that enrollments in Fairfax County economics courses were dismal during the early 1980s. There were only seven semester-length sections of economics taught in all 21 high schools, with as few as a dozen students in each section.

The Applied Economics Program

Therefore, I welcomed the news in 1983 about Junior Achievement's Applied Economics (AE) Program, which I understood contained a computer component. Although my closest encounter with a computer until that time had been my bank's "Money Exchange," I felt that the existence of a computer in my classroom would accomplish two goals. First, I hoped that computer-based activities might be an attraction to students and help reverse the trend toward declining enrollments. Second, I believed that the computer would contribute to technological literacy, both mine and my students'.

There are five facets of my experience with AE and Junior Achievement that may be of interest to other teachers: (1) what happened in my economics classroom as a result of the introduction of an activity-centered curriculum, (2) the potential for computer components in social studies curriculum, (3) my experience with business/education partnerships, (4) my involvement in a dynamic team approach to curriculum development, and (5) how the Information Age is likely to affect teaching.

If students are to be exposed to the benefits of economics training, then they must register for the course. AE's activity-centered curriculum has proven to be an effective inducement. Enrollments in my own classes and those through-out the county have quadrupled since AE was introduced.

AE combines a text and study guide with several structured activities, includ-ing the formation of a student-run company and computer-based simulations, that allow students to apply economic theory in practical ways. The course sponsor, a local business, donates money to cover the cost of materials and provides a consultant who makes one-day-a-week classroom visits. The AE curriculum is also the first in social studies to include specific technological literacy objectives.

"The Big Kahuna" is one illustration of how AE activities engage students. In the spring of 1987, my AE class formed a company called The Big Kahuna. When we held an election for company officers, the seniors formed a powerful coalition to elect a serious-minded sophomore as president. Under his leader-ship, the company decided to design and purchase T-shirts that commemorated "Beach Week 1987" (it is a school tradition for seniors to spend the week following graduation at the beach).

Each member of the class contributed to capitalization by selling stock in the company. Artists were located among the student body who provided prelim-inary designs. Final designs were selected by a class vote, and a screen printing house was found to produce the shirts. Market research was conducted to determine an optimal combination of price and quantity, and differing budget assumptions were tested with the aid of computer software. A bank account was opened, and financial records were generated both on paper and by using the financial applications software that has been specially designed for the course.

Even though the company encountered a few difficulties in getting timely delivery of the product, all the shirts were sold within a week after we received them. Class members voted themselves and the artists healthy bonuses, paid the stockholders a 600 percent return, and donated the remaining profits toward the purchase of another computer for future AE classes. My business consultant for AE, an IBM employee who assists me throughout the course, helped the students liquidate their company.

Encouraging Student Participation

This is the kind of activity that students thoroughly enjoy—one that is nonthreatening and encourages all members of the class to participate. The student-run company creates additional work for the teacher, but the extra work doesn't become a problem if the consultant is employed effectively. Enthusiasm for the course spreads by word of mouth, making the task of engaging students in the study of economics that much easier when a new class begins.

Although the student-run company is an important part of AE, it is by no means the only structured activity used in the course. Applied Economics was the first major social studies program to integrate computer-based activities into its curriculum. In fact, one of the more interesting features of my associ-ation with AE is the opportunity it has provided for work with advanced technology in the classroom. Of the several applications of computers used in the course, which include word processing, electronic spread sheets, and accounting programs, I believe simulations are the most interesting and promising. Computer-based simulations have the power to engage students in learning by placing them in a risk-free, experiential environment.

One of the pieces of AE software, for example, simulates various aspects of the operation of a company, including budgeting, ordering parts, producing products, and developing a marketing strategy. The production process is especially interesting. The program presents student teams with a production screen, a computer-generated factory in which teams assemble finished products. As the teams engage this screen, they experiment with the goal of increasing productivity. Since the teams are charged a wage-rate-per-worker-per-minute, the results of various experiments rapidly become apparent in daily reports and financial statements.

After students have had three or four rounds of experimentation I can use their experience, and together we can discover several principles of economics (total product; increasing, diminishing, and negative returns; marginal product; productivity). Again, drawing on their experience, my students can describe the assumptions behind each of these principles. One of these assumptions (that technology is fixed) can be changed by varying the speed of elements in the production process. After more experimentation, students begin to understand the relationship between technology and productivity.

This simulation also contains a specially designed word processing program, which is included to give students some experience with the technology. Teams use the word processor to type and print company slogans and marketing plans. I use these plans to evaluate student understanding of the textbook.

Simulation with Student Teams

A simulation I use during the second half of the course pits student teams against one another in a computer-controlled market. A round in this simulation is completed when all teams have entered their decisions about price and production and how much to spend on marketing, research and development, and investment in plant and equipment. The computer program, which contains a complex set of interrelated equations, calculates the market share for each team; prepares financial and market reports aggregated for the industry and disaggregated for each team; and displays this information on-screen, all within a matter of seconds after the last team has entered its decisions.

Even though this simulation is a good way for me to review and reinforce concepts from the theory of price, its main utility is found in its relationship to macroeconomics. There is embedded within the program a "teacher-control" function, through which I can create a business cycle. It is interesting to see how quickly students adopt what I can only call a recession mentality when they reach that part of the cycle and how difficult it is for them to change when conditions improve. Discussions of government countercyclical policies are enriched and enlivened after students have had the experience of "living through" a recession.

When I use these simulations, my classroom becomes a laboratory. Student behavior and experience lead them to the discovery of important concepts and principles of economics. These principles are defined and the assumptions behind them are clarified. Of greater importance, however, is that the teaching methods engage students in the study of economics, and students must use vital skills to learn the subject matter.

The Awakening of Corporate Citizenship

Yet another benefit resulting from participation with AE has been an awakening toward the business community. There has been a freshening sense of corporate citizenship throughout the 1980s. AE has given me a glimpse of the potential for, and the barriers to, cooperation with the private sector.

One concept that has been a product of my collaboration with the business community evolved over time through discussions with Dr. Peter Harder, the Junior Achievement vice president who created and managed the AE curriculum development process. That idea, actually borrowed from the practice of many large corporations, is "intrapreneurship." When applied to education, intrapreneurship means providing teams of educators with appropriate resources to foster the design and development of curriculum. An intrapreneurship program brings teachers together, not only with specialists in learning theory and curriculum design but also with other experts, such as computer programmers, to develop and implement curriculum projects.

The Writing/Reasoning Achievement Project (WRAP) was my first attempt to initiate an intrapreneurship program within my school system. Like any high school, mine has a population of at-risk students. The idea behind WRAP was to develop an interdisciplinary approach for these students that would include mathematics, English, and social studies as a core, as well as guidance and career awareness components. Teachers, guidance counselors, and administrators at the school, sensitive to the special needs of this type of student, were enthusiastic about the plan.

My work with the private sector in connection with AE encouraged me to approach local business leaders with the WRAP idea. Those leaders, who had already formed a foundation to support the public schools, were interested in participating in the WRAP experiment. The education department at George Mason University, located in Fairfax County, also offered its expertise to aid the project.

Even though we managed to move the project to this stage, it faltered because the school system is not suitably organized to support large-scale, school-based curriculum development projects. One wise old turk from the county's Department of Instruction, who incidentally had never heard me use the term 'intrapreneurship,' reminded me, as negotiations for the project unraveled, that "a school system is no place for entrepreneurs." Even so, the original team of teachers and counselors maintains its interest, and the business community is about to establish a grant program to support this kind of project.

WRAP in many ways sought to replicate my experience with the AE curriculum development process. That process, as I have said, was the brainchild of Pete Harder. Dr. Harder assembled a committee of business leaders, economists, teachers, and curriculum specialists to define course goals. He later recruited and led a team that was charged with designing and integrating activities into a unified program of study. The team included teachers, authors, content and curriculum specialists, and computer programmers. The team's success can be traced both to the fact that sufficient resources were provided for the effort and to the synergy that developed among team members whose skills were complementary.

I think that another key to the success of this process is that it was organized to receive and act upon suggestions from teachers who were using the materials. Surveys and other evaluation instruments revealed what worked and what did not. The design team acted upon these suggestions. The dynamic, teacher-centered team process used to develop AE is especially significant to the special demands of the Information Age. As technology is integrated into curriculum, this kind of development process will become increasingly necessary.

Technology and the Nature of Teaching

Technology is destined to change the nature of teaching. Word processing systems and electronic spread sheet applications have already increased teacher productivity. Tests, worksheets, and other teacher-prepared materials can be created, edited, and saved for future use. The ease with which these materials can be revised frees teachers for enhancing their quality.

Other productivity software is presently being developed. In AE, for example, I have access to a "test generator" program. I simply specify how many questions I desire, at what degree of difficulty, from which chapters in the text. The computer program then randomly selects appropriate items from a "bank" of test questions, and automatically prints a complete test.

Many social studies teachers and curriculum developers are experimenting with data base management systems. When we become more sophisticated in the use of telecommunications, schools will have access to literally thousands of data bases. The research process will change dramatically as "search strategies" become an indispensable skill for all citizens to acquire.

The introduction of networking will change schools and the classroom. Schoolwide networks will give teachers instant access to student records. Recording attendance and grades will consume far less time than today, creating the possibility for more anecdotal record keeping and better sharing of information among teachers. Networks within the classroom will enhance the quality of computer-based activities and, thereby, fundamentally alter student/teacher interaction.

The Technological Revolution presents our education system with its greatest challenge in history. We have much to do. Our school calendars are remnants of an Agrarian Age, our bureaucracies and curricula are suited to an Industrial Age, and our students will become adults in an Information Age.

The social studies have a vital role to play in meeting this challenge. The quality of tomorrow's citizens depends on our success at adapting the curriculum so that it is responsive to emerging requirements. To the mission of transmitting cultural knowledge, we must, for example, add technological literacy objectives. Charles White (1987) is correct when he observes:

Education for effective democratic citizenship must include both knowledge and skills. With respect to the latter, students must receive explicit training in information processing skills.

The experiences I have had in working with Junior Achievement while implementing the Applied Economics course in my classroom have given me both a blueprint for effective curriculum design and a vision of the future. Experienced, creative educators, when provided sufficient financial and technical resources, can develop highly innovative curricula that truly engage students in learning. Technology, whether used to enhance teacher productivity or integrated into curriculum, fundamentally alters virtually every aspect of education.

The Information Age will put tremendous strains on social studies teachers. Much of the knowledge and many of the skills with which we have become comfortable are rapidly becoming obsolete. We must replace this obsolete base and do it quickly.

The turbulence we are encountering at the threshold of the Information Age is disturbing. Society, unnerved by this discord, has turned to social studies teachers both to explain the present and to prepare our young for the future. What we do with this mandate, whether we do it well or poorly, will have a profound effect on that future. What a great time to be teaching social studies!

REFERENCES

Bloom, Allan. *The Closing of the American Mind.* New York: Simon and Schuster, 1987.

Carnegie Task Force on Teaching as a Profession. *A Nation Prepared: Teachers for the 21st Century.* New York: Carnegie Forum on Education and the Economy, 1986.

Hirsch, E.D., Jr. *Cultural Literacy: What Every American Needs to Know.* Boston: Houghton Mifflin, 1987.

King, David C. "Delay Persists in Social Studies Reform, But Signs Point to Headway Just Ahead," *ASCD Curriculum Update,* August 1987.

National Endowment for the Humanities. *American Memory: A Report on the Humanities in the Nation's Public Schools.* Washington, D.C.: National Endowment for the Humanities, 1987.

White, Charles S. "Democratic Citizenship and Information Technology: Promises, Challenges, and Remedies." Paper presented at the 50th Anniversary Conference of the American Society for Information Science, Boston, Massachusetts, October 5, 1987.

CONCLUDING COMMENTS

Sara Lawrence Lightfoot's book, *The Good High School,** is arguably one of the most important, provocative, and influential books published on American education during the last decade. Subtitled *Portraits of Excellence*, Lightfoot decided to study six American high schools that, by every indicator, were succeeding. Parents, school board members, and a variety of community leaders all thought so—and so did teachers and students. In general, dropout rates were low, test scores were high, and the needs of students of varying abilities and different racial and ethnic backgrounds were being met. As she studied each school, Lightfoot focused on the question, "If these schools were indeed as good as they seemed to be, *why* and *how* were they good?"

We owe Lightfoot a debt of gratitude, since she inspired the approach we decided to take in this bulletin. Our overriding purpose was to provide social studies teachers with ideas, information, and inspiration to enable them to improve the effectiveness of their teaching. It seemed clear to us that one way to do this was to identify good teachers and let them speak for themselves through detailed descriptions of their work.

Our contributors have written eloquently about their experiences. We think they have made an enormously important contribution to the field by doing so; for that we thank them.

It remains for us, the editors, to complete the cycle by raising Lightfoot's question in this new context—that is, as we examine the work of eleven outstanding social studies teachers, can we gain some insight into why and how they were good? Do they have characteristics in common? Dare we generalize about good social studies teachers?

We think we can. Our authors teach at every grade level—kindergarten through high school. They teach in public and in independent schools, in urban and in rural settings, on the east and west coasts and in between. They teach blacks, whites, Hispanics, and Asians; they teach the bright and the slow, privileged and disadvantaged. All these teachers are, of course, uniquely themselves: idiosyncratic, spontaneous, creative, different in a number of ways from other teachers.

Some Common Qualities

At the same time, however, we were able to discern some common qualities that seemed to transcend their differences. As we read and reread their contributions, it became clear that these good teachers share important notions about what makes for effective social studies teaching. The remainder of this section outlines what seemed to us the most important of those commonalities.

To begin with, all our teachers had a clear sense of *purpose* in their work that went far beyond the listing of narrow, relatively low-level objectives. They seem to have internalized ideas that others talk about glibly, but rarely apply—that students can, indeed, learn to respect and value differences among human

---

*Sara Lawrence Lightfoot, *The Good High School* (New York: Basic Books, 1983).

beings; that such values as freedom, justice, and equality are more than abstract principles; they can be taught, and what is more important, they can be lived on a day-to-day basis in school classrooms; if social studies are to teach responsible citizenship, then students must take and carry out responsibility. It seems fair to conclude that these teachers will not miss the forest for the trees. They know where they are going, why they are teaching history, anthropology, economics, or current affairs. This sense of purpose guides their work, gives it meaning, direction, and significance in the larger scheme of things.

Closely related to this point, our teachers *themselves* care deeply about the issues they and their students study. They are not robots in a moral vacuum to whom one subject or topic in the curriculum guide is the same as any other. They care—sometimes passionately—about what happens to the land we live on, for example. Environmental and other concerns are not merely textbook titles; they are part of the emotional and intellectual makeup of the good teachers who have written for this bulletin.

Our contributors have given an enormous amount of thought to the importance of process as well as product in the act of teaching. Students are consistently asked to think; they observe, interview, gather and analyze data, search, inquire, compare, reflect, create, collaborate, decide, debate, argue, represent, and share ideas. In short, these teachers put flesh on the bones of the many exhortations to think that teachers are bombarded with today. The children in our teacher's classrooms do think; they do so naturally, as part of everyday classroom activity, and they generally do so in context rather than in isolated exercises.

We have been struck by the importance our teacher-writers place on content—the facts, concepts, and generalizations that make up much of the stuff of social studies. Although process is indeed important, all our contributors recognize that neither research nor other skills are taught or learned in a vacuum. One must think about something; our teachers clearly define what that something is. "Content" is not for them a dirty word; on the contrary, *what* is studied may be as important as *how* it is studied. From Caroline Donnan's 3d grade study of local history to Michael Rossi's high school course on The American Experience, our writers were concerned with ideas of significance and enduring value.

Significantly, these teachers appear to have mastered the ability to blend knowledge, thought, and feeling in their work. The artificial separation of product and process is rejected. Our authors may teach an academic subject—sociology, for example—but they also help students work with information to analyze the accuracy and value of that information. Moreover, they ask students to consider the potential impact of their conclusions: "If this is true, what follows, how do I feel about that, why do I feel that way, should I try to change the situation or should I change my attitude, how *can* I change the situation, and what else do I need to know? The loops of thinking, information, and values are interconnected. Each question and answer have implications for knowledge, thought, and feeling. These authors seem comfortable with this blend.

Teachers As Autonomous Curriculum Builders

Another characteristic shared by all our contributors was their willingness to depart from formal curricular guidelines and go their own way as the situation demanded to become autonomous curriculum *builders.* Our teachers showed a great deal of courage as they broke new ground in their attempts to develop lively, engaging, reality-based studies for their students. They are clearly risk-takers, willing to take chances and try new ways, topics, or subjects. Pauline Dyson's comparative study of black family life, for example, took courage to develop and carry out, as did Betsy Dudley's creation of a functional class constitution.

What is perhaps more important, all our teachers taught in schools or school systems where independence on the part of skilled teachers was encouraged. These teachers flourished in a nurturing, supportive climate which allowed them to be creative, resourceful, and daring curriculum builders.

Our reading of these classroom portraits revealed other commonalities as well. It seemed clear to us that, for these teachers, "less was indeed more," to borrow Ted Sizer's phrase. The quality work they produced took time, and they were willing to take the time to dig into their work in some depth, rather than to skim superficially over information to cover the curriculum.

They used this time well, moreover, to plan and organize their ideas and materials so that students gained confidence in their own knowledge and ability to learn. Kevin O'Reilly's work with thinking skills reminds us that a few higher-level, Bloom-taxonomic-like cognitive questions will not teach students how to think. The work needs careful planning and structuring of materials to enable students to see both the need for and means necessary for thought.

Our teachers seem also to have internalized an essential understanding about the nature of information. One can see information either as facts or as evidence. In the former case, *facts* are separate, fragmented pieces that we frequently ask students to memorize. *Evidence* is information logically related to other information to explain, compare, or evaluate. Evidence is information *in service* to learning—a centerpiece of the work of the teachers represented in this bulletin.

Our teachers ranged widely, but not wildly, in their use of both methods and materials. Included in these pages are descriptions of field trips, journal keeping, role-playing, simulation, peer teaching, and creative imagery. They borrowed ideas from others, sometimes collaborating in teaching teams. In addition, they incorporated the work of other disciplines in their activities, crossing the traditional boundaries of history and social studies to include art, music, architecture, religion, drama, literature, or folklore. For these teachers, method and materials were everywhere.

Jean Piaget observed that one has not learned something until he or she has "acted upon it," i.e., done something with what has been studied—explained it to someone else, transformed it in some way. The good teachers we invited to contribute to this bulletin seem to have internalized this idea. They encourage students to do far more than merely absorb information. Students use, analyze, and reflect upon knowledge. Knowledge has *meaning* for them. Perhaps this conception of the nature of learning lies at the heart of the excellence they have displayed as they have generously shared their work with all of us.

Vincent Rogers
Arthur D. Roberts
Thomas P. Weinland